TO THE GLORY OF ALMIGHTY GOD:

Father, Son and Holy Spirit

and

In honour of my father,

JOHN OHWOFASA OGEFERE *JP*

My Diary of Down Upside Prayers

Book One

DEBORAH OGEFERE-ONYEKWULUJE

SYNCTERFACE™
Syncterface Media
London
www.syncterfacemedia.com

My Diary of Upside Down Prayers
ISBN: 978-0-9569741-5-0
Copyright © January 2013
Deborah Ogefere-Onyekwuluje
All Rights Reserved

Published in the United Kingdom by

Syncterface Media
London
www.syncterfacemedia.com
info@syncterfacemedia.com

Cover Design: Syncterface Media, London

This book is printed on acid-free paper

CONTENTS

ACKNOWLEDGEMENTS

I am grateful to Julie and Bill Croydon who read the initial manuscript and made many useful suggestions and amendments. Their insightful comments helped shape this book.

I am also appreciative of the support of friends like Timmy Makanju, who since hearing about the book has not ceased to encourage me. That this book has been published is partly down to his push. I wish to thank my friend, Oby Anubi for sharing the vision, and for her words of encouragement and support. A big thank you also goes to Barbara Noresa Staph for always being there for me.

No book can be written without the support, and sometimes sacrifice, of one's family. I thank my husband, Dr Achike Onyekwuluje and my three children, Achike (Jnr), Chioma and Chudi for their patience, encouragement and support while I was writing this book.

Finally, I am indebted to Akin Olunloyo and the team at Syncterface Media for their support and hard work in getting this book published. Thank you!

INTRODUCTION

Dear Reader,

Welcome to the country called Upside Down. Before you go ahead and read this little diary of mine, there are a few things I would like to make you aware of. In Upside Down country...

- You may ask any person of the Holy Trinity: Father, Son and Holy Spirit, any question you like, especially those tricky ones that no one will answer in church because of their uncomfortable nature.

- Almighty God will answer your questions, and if you listen as carefully as I did, you will hear Him loud and clear. However, bear in mind that, though His answers may not be what you want to hear, they will always be in line with what is written in His holy textbook, the Bible; He will always answer and speak for Himself.

- You should try as much as possible to know your scriptures because each person of the Holy Trinity knows the scriptures upside down, inside out, back to front, wrong way round and right way up. So if you must quote scripture make sure you do not quote it out of context. If you do, Holy Spirit will make you re-learn the entire bible.

- Do not allow the Holy Teacher - oops, Holy

Spirit, to catch you out on a question you have asked. If you do you will be forced to do some research.

- You may ask any question within or outside the Christian faith but do not allow your research to take you too far into enemy territory. Do enough to get the basic knowledge and understanding.

- Whatever you do, be relaxed with Almighty God. He does not bite and He does not take offence. He loves you very much and His only agenda is to see you conformed to the image of His Son, Jesus. Feel free to speak Upside Down language to Him at any time; He understands it perfectly and probably prefers it to some of those long prayers we pray.

- The following are the entry requirements to the land of Upside Down:
  - Passport – Lord Jesus
  - Visa – Holy Spirit
  - Destination – Heaven; abode of Heavenly Father

Good luck as you find your way around Upside Down country. Enjoy the laughs, enjoy the knowledge; enjoy the wisdom and enjoy the general information that awaits you; some of it useful, some of it not. The goal is simply to relax and enjoy the presence of Almighty God.

January 5
FORGIVENESS

Heavenly Father asked me to forgive someone who hurt, and continues to hurt, me. I was quite reluctant to do this so I told Him:

DEBBIE: My eyes are not Your eyes, neither are Your ways my ways.

HEAVENLY FATHER: Jesus, Holy Spirit, is this quote in the bible? I do not recollect it.

HOLY SPIRIT: It is an Upside Down quote of Isaiah 55:8. As You will soon find out, Debbie has a habit of quoting scripture upside down to suit her.

Heavenly Father turned His gaze to Debbie.

HEAVENLY FATHER: So Debbie My dear daughter, what is this your way that I do not know of?

DEBBIE: You see from above, I see from below and what I see I do not like! You have the eyes of eternity and from the beginning You know the end. I only see a snapshot of a person's life. You are divine, I am human and I can no longer endure the pain that I am being subjected to. However, I concede that Your ways are perfect, therefore I forgive.

Father, forgive us our sins as we forgive those who sin against us.

January 10
I WANT IT NOW!

My friend Becky is in the habit of telling me that my reward is in heaven each time I do something good. In fact, she says it so often that at the rate she is going, I am beginning to think that I will have more rewards in heaven than here on earth. So, I decided to talk to my Saviour about it:

DEBBIE: Lord Jesus, You know all those rewards that I have piled up in heaven? Well, I was wondering if I could have some of them credited to my earthly account. I see no point in being in the red down here on earth, when my heavenly account is over flowing! I am sure this is a simple transaction which should not take too long.

This question seemed to catch Lord Jesus unawares. He decided to consult Heavenly Father.

LORD JESUS: Heavenly Father, how do We carry out this transaction? Do heaven and earth share the same currency?

Heavenly Father scratched His holy head and looked on in amazement.

HEAVENLY FATHER: This is a job for Holy Spirit. "Holy Spirit, how do We do this?"

Holy Spirit was silent; Lord Jesus was getting a bit anxious.

LORD JESUS: Holy Spirit, say or do something!

HOLY SPIRIT: I am thinking, or should I say, meditating?

What I thought to be a simple and straight forward request seemed to be giving Almighty God some food for thought. Perhaps, I should inform all my Christian brothers and sisters to make similar requests. This should keep Holy Spirit busy. Just think of all the transactions the angels will have to carry out; enough to close down a few national bank accounts.

Anyway, that is not my problem; my job is to simply put in my request. After all, the bible does say, "Be anxious for nothing, but in everything, make your requests known to God". (For those of you in the know, this is not the exact quote; it is a case of editing scripture to suit me!).

Just when I thought I had everything wrapped up, Heavenly Father clapped His hands; heaven heaved a sigh of relief...

HEAVENLY FATHER: Jesus, Holy Spirit, I have caught her in her own cleverness.

Debbie, my dear daughter, what am I to do about those times when I gave you advice and wisdom; those times when I guided you and told you what to do? To whom should I send my legal and consultation bill?

LORD JESUS: Debbie, my dear friend, what about those times when I rescued you; when I saw you through difficult times; when I carried you through the storms of life; when I cared for you and nurtured you? To whom should I send my bill?

HOLY SPIRIT: Debbie, my clever pupil, what about those times when I healed you; those times when I comforted you and pointed you in the right direction? To whom should I send my bill? How do you intend to pay back? Oh, and by the way, I would prefer my payment in heaven!

HEAVENLY FATHER: My dear Debbie, do you want Us to continue or do you need time to meditate on your folly?

Suddenly a, holy terror gripped my heart; I had been caught out. I pondered what to do. Where would I get the means to pay Almighty God what I owed Him? On second thoughts, maybe it would be better for my heavenly reward to remain in heaven! At this point I quickly withdrew my claim.

Here is my advice to all my brothers and sisters who are thinking of following in my footsteps: Withdraw before it is too late as it is impossible to settle any bill issued by Holy Trinity!

As for those of you who are not yet Christians, your situation is slightly more dire. How do you plan to earn salvation? What good works do you intend to do to satisfy Almighty God? If I were you I would take the easy option and embrace Christ as Saviour. This single act alone will wipe your slate clean and reconcile you with your Heavenly Father.

Jesus is the way, the truth and the life (John 14:6). "Nor is there salvation in any other, for there is no other name under heaven given among men by which we must be saved." (Acts 4:12)

NEVER DOUBT HIS PROMISES

I was thanking and praising my Heavenly Father for my family and His promise to bless. Suddenly I felt Him test me when a thought flashed through my mind, "What if none of these things came to pass?"

DEBBIE: Heavenly Father, I guess You know this already, but I do know, and can quote certain scripture verses.

I brought out my bible, opened it to the book of Numbers Chapter 23 verse 19:

DEBBIE: "God is not a man, that He should lie, nor a son of man, that He should repent. Has He said, and will He not do? Or has He spoken, and will He not make it good?" Heavenly Father, You really should not have tested me. Lord Jesus knows that I know the scripture upside down and back to front. Holy Spirit should have told you that I know my scriptures the right way up too!

After quoting this verse I was almost certain that Heavenly Father would be sorry that He had allowed this scripture to be written in the bible. I went on to quote another scripture to Him; this time back to front…

DEBBIE: All scripture is good for reminding God of His promises, just in case He forgets". (*But we all know that God does not forget!*).

I left Heavenly Father to ponder whether He would issue a decree to delete this scripture from the book of Numbers.

Long after I had forgotten this conversation I heard…

HEAVENLY FATHER: I am going to take charge and carry out an inquiry. First, how did Numbers 23:19 find its way into My book?

Both the Holy Spirit and Lord Jesus looked at Heavenly Father.

LORD JESUS: Father, if we go down this road, Debbie will only dig out more scripture verses like Matthew 24:35 that just might leave Us homeless: "Heaven and earth will pass away but My words will by no means pass away"!

HOLY SPIRIT: The secret is out. The word is written; it has been spoken and claimed, and has been used to remind Us! So, as You can see, this line of inquiry will profit Us nothing.

Heavenly Father had no choice but to agree.

HEAVENLY FATHER: Ok, so who tested Debbie?

HOLY SPIRIT: Search Me; I normally test for other things.

LORD JESUS: Certainly not I.

HEAVENLY FATHER: And it definitely was not Me. So, who in heaven, earth or hell tested my daughter?

Lord Jesus, who has comprehensive experience in several realms – on earth, heaven and in the land of the dead, decided to shed some light…

LORD JESUS: It could be that the test was designed in hell by the enemy gang leader; Satan himself.

As soon as I heard this, the penny dropped. I knew that I was in the wrong, again. How could I think that my Heavenly Father would cause me to doubt His promises? I repented in dust and ashes.

LORD JESUS: Debbie, as you seem to be so clever, could you kindly show Me in the scriptures where Heavenly Father caused anyone to doubt His promises?

I did a quick mental flip through the bible but I could not think of a single verse. I was sincerely repentant, but at the same time I was furious with myself. How could I have thought such a thing about my Heavenly Father? I should have known that this was the work of the father of all doubters, Satan himself.

DEBBIE: Heavenly Father, I am so, so sorry.

LORD JESUS: Take consolation Debbie. In hindsight you never really doubted. You actually responded in faith using the most appropriate scripture you could lay your hands on.

Now, that cheered me up a little.

HOLY SPIRIT: Heavenly Father, now that she has repented, please release the blessing before she quotes another one of those scriptures that Your Ancient of Days mind might find a bit hard to comprehend and I will be forced to teach You.

Heavenly Father briefly pondered the prospect of going for a crash course at the school of the Holy Spirit. Then He shook His head and said to Himself, "That is not an option; it will definitely not do My holy reputation any good!"

LORD JESUS: Heavenly Father, this is an awkward situation; *kuku*[1] release the blessings, and avoid further embarrassment. Hide Yourself!

Heavenly Father clapped His hands and summoned the angels.

HEAVENLY FATHER: Angels, let the blessings flow.

There was a big sigh of relief in heaven and the angels, and the saints resumed praise.

God will not cause you to doubt His promises for He has said that His word will not return to Him void, but it shall accomplish what He pleases and prosper in the thing for which He sent it. (Isaiah 55:11). So, have faith and wait patiently for the Lord, He will never let you down

THE GIFT OF IMAGINATION

I was about to embark on a massive project and I found myself wondering how to go about it. In despair I thought to myself, "I know I lack imagination and I could really do with the gift of imagination". Unknown to me, Almighty God was listening:

HEAVENLY FATHER: Should We leave her with her ideas or should We lend a helping hand?

LORD JESUS: Leave this with Me Heavenly Father, I will handle it.

So Debbie My dear servant, I hear that in addition to all the gifts of the Holy Spirit you also want the gift of imagination, do you? Tell Me, who in the bible has this gift?"

I thought about this a little then cheekily responded...

DEBBIE: Joseph, no? Daniel, no? Aha, I've got it: Apostle John, yes?

LORD JESUS: No! No!! No!!! It appears that among other things you also need the gift of memorising and remembering scriptures.

Now that would be a good gift to have, I thought.

LORD JESUS: And while you are at it you might also want to ask Holy Spirit for the gift of tying shoe laces and knotting ties.

Then I saw His point and had to concede that there really is no such thing as the gift of imagination or the gift of memorising scripture.

Holy Spirit: Lazy *pikin*[2], wait for Me, I am coming to help you move your fingers and write down your ideas!

There is no such thing as the gift of imagination or the gift of memorising scripture. Everyone has an imagination; use yours to bless your Creator. Also, anyone can memorise scripture. All you need to do is set your mind to it.

February 23
SALVATION

Debbie: Lord Jesus!

Lord Jesus: Yes Debbie, I hope I have not done anything wrong, like break any of your Upside Down rules?

Debbie: Not really, I just want a quiet word. I think I've made a mistake.

Lord Jesus: What mistake might that be, Debbie?

Debbie: I made the decision to put my faith in You way too early in life. I think I should have followed the example of the thief at Calvary who repented of his sins and gave his life to You just when he was about to die.

Lord Jesus was speechless, probably meditating His response to what I just said. Then I heard...

Holy Spirit: Should I expel this cheeky girl from My school?

Heavenly Father: Wait, she may yet repent in dust and ashes.

Lord Jesus: Debbie you are so sharp that one day you will cut yourself. So, now you are thinking of giving your life to Me on your death bed are you?

Somehow I forgot to think before answering...

Debbie: Yes, that is what I have in mind.

The angels and saints in heaven were flabbergasted.

LORD JESUS: My very clever friend Debbie, tell Me how will you know the time and manner of your death? What makes you think that you will be in a position to make the decision to follow Me at that time?

I had to admit that I had not thought this through. Once again I saw the error in my thinking. I thanked Almighty God that I had already embraced Jesus as my Lord and Saviour and my eternal destination is settled.

Should I die anytime from now, it would be a case of, **"Go directly to heaven, do not stop to check how hot it is in hell; do not stop to check how many souls are stranded in Purgatory, if such a place exists; go directly to the Pearly Gates of Heaven where Saint Peter and the angels are waiting to usher you in!"**

The angels and saints in heaven chorused a resounding, "AMEN!"

By the way, this goes for all residents of Upside Down who have met the entry requirements. (See Introduction)

It is never too early in life to put your faith in Christ and choose to follow Him for *"Behold, now is the accepted time; behold, now is the day of salvation"* (2 Corinthians 6:2). So, do not delay! Also, if your relationship with Jesus has taken a dive in the wrong direction and you have backslidden, it is not too late to put things right. Return to Him and "Today, if you will hear His voice: Do not harden your hearts" (Psalm 95:7-8)

February 27
KNOW THE WORD

A friend phoned to ask if I knew the scripture reference for a quote she had in mind. I told her that although I did not know the exact chapter and verse, I did know the scripture by heart. So I proceeded to quote it to her correctly. She was so shocked that I did not know where this scripture was in the bible, especially as I have a reputation of knowing a lot of scripture verses. Well, I eventually used my concordance and was finally able to give her the correct reference.

Sometime after this I heard…

LORD JESUS: I keep telling you that you need to sharpen your scripture referencing. You know how to quote scriptures back to front, inside out and upside down but you never seem to know where to find them in the bible. As you can see, today such an effort would have yielded dividends.

I was silent; I knew Lord Jesus was right. But after a moment of meditation a light bulb went off in my head...

DEBBIE: Gotcha! Own goal, Heavenly Father blow the whistle!

Lord Jesus, out of curiosity, how often did You give the chapter and verse when You quoted scripture? Did You not just quote it and leave the person to find where it was referenced? Well, I am only following in Your footsteps.

This time the Lord Jesus was silent. I think I really got Him here. I could even hear Heavenly Father and Holy Spirit burst out in a roar of laughter.

HEAVENLY FATHER: Jesus, You were so busy abiding that You failed to notice what We discerned a long time ago. Debbie is a trouble maker and so Holy Spirit and I decided to put on our most loving and comforting behaviour when dealing with her. Why do You think I pamper her so much? I would advise that You change Your approach.

I left Lord Jesus to meditate on how best to pamper me!

The bible was given to change us. It is more important for you to make sure that you allow the truth in the bible to change you so that you become the person God destined you to be, than to just quote its chapters and verses.

March 20
UPSIDE DOWN PRAISE

DEBBIE: Heavenly Father are You sitting comfortably on Your throne because I am about to praise You?

HEAVENLY FATHER: This is a rarity Debbie my daughter. I better enjoy it.

DEBBIE: Heavenly Father You are so **loving, caring,** and **compassionate** and there is absolutely no father like You. If it were possible, I would ask You to increase Your love for me but I know You love me unconditionally.

You are **all-powerful** and many of us know, and have experienced this aspect of your character in our lives. But when was the last time You moved in power such that the whole world acknowledged it was You? When was the last time mankind quaked in fear at the thought of facing You? Will we ever witness a repeat of the events on Mount Sinai in our generation? Many actually think it is just a made-up story.

The writing of Your commandments on the tablets of our hearts is taking way too long. Is it not possible to save them on a computer chip that can be inserted into our brains at say, the age of five? Then when we grow older, we would automatically know Your commandments. All this reading, memorising and meditating on scripture just ain't working. We need a shortcut. As You know, we are an 'instant' generation; we want everything done pronto. Heavenly Father, You need to move with the times.

As for Your **mercy, grace** and **forgiveness**; a few of us believe that You are just too merciful and forgiving, except of course when we are on the receiving end. But seriously speaking, mankind is beginning to take Your mercy and grace for granted. Some see it as a sign of weakness and even blaspheme Your holy name because they think nothing will happen.

I could discern that all was not quite right with what I had just told Heavenly Father. It was time to offer praise to Lord Jesus.

Debbie: Lord Jesus, did You know that some brave and very wise people, at least wise in their own eyes, have decided that they do not need a **Saviour** or a **Redeemer**? They believe that they can save themselves. And as for You being their **Righteousness**; they believe that their good deeds are enough to present them as holy before Heavenly Father. Judging by the way they are going, it is obvious that they no longer need You to intercede on their behalf because they can save themselves.

We, that is my faithful brothers and sisters as well as myself, take You at Your word. We know that "You are the **Way**, the **Truth** and the **Life**" and no one comes to the Father except through You. However, we are now being told that all roads lead to God. So what is the point of following You?

Lord Jesus, the fact that You are **all-knowing** kind of scares us, especially as a few of us wish there were some things You did not know about us. You are **all-wise** and we wish we knew at birth that we could tap into Your endless wisdom. This would have saved a lot of heartache and pain.

As for being **all-powerful**; we want You to blaze forth.

Let a few mountains quake at the sound of Your voice. We, that is a few of us Christians, know You are the **Judge of the earth** but so far it is hard to see any evidence. Why not move in power and claim Your inheritance; What are You waiting for? If you do nothing now, it just might be too late by the time of Your second coming. Show Your power and let all the world leaders know who is in charge! You would be making life much easier for us Christians.

And Lord Jesus, just in case you have not noticed, many religious walls of Jericho have sprung up all around the world. We Christians are being told that we may not call upon You, or proclaim You, or even worship You in certain parts of the world. In short, You, the **King of kings** and the **Lord of lords**, have been barred from, and are no longer welcome in some parts of the earth. I just do not understand how the **King of glory**, through whom and for whom all things were created may not go anywhere He pleases within His very own creation.

While the Lord Jesus pondered what to make of my praise I decided to turn my attention to Holy Spirit.

DEBBIE: Holy Spirit, I love you dearly especially because You are so **loving, caring, compassionate, gracious** and **kind**. Some of us love You as our **teacher, counsellor** and **guide**. However, even though many of us will not admit it, we are not all fans of Your teaching methods. I mean, no one ever graduates from Your school, and I would not be surprised if when we get to heaven You still have something to teach us.

As for Your gifts, we love them but we do not understand why You allow them to be counterfeited such that non-servants of Christ also seem to perform dubious healings and give false prophecies. Is it not time You moved in power and confiscated all spiritual gifts not given by You? I mean, why do You allow miracles that do not originate from You?

I am sure that You have also noticed that the prophets and prophetesses of modern day Baal are on the increase. Many of them even claim that You are the source of their power and regularly take advantage of the gullible. We have no doubt that You are **all-knowing, all-wise** and **all-powerful**, but when was the last time you moved in power in our midst such that the whole world stopped to take stock? When are You going to engineer another showdown with these prophets of false religions, cults and sects? It is about time we had an updated version of Elijah and the prophets of Baal!

That was all my praise for the Holy Spirit. I thought it would be a good idea to round up by offering a bit more praise to Heavenly Father.

DEBBIE: Dear Heavenly Father, it is me again. I was wondering, what are You going to do about the landmines, atomic weapons and nuclear warheads; all these so-called weapons of technological advancement and mass destruction that will only end up taking us down? Could You not give us insight on how to avoid a nuclear holocaust before we blow up the earth which You gave us? The rate at which we are going, these weapons could end up blowing up the heavens and all the planets in the solar system!

To end my praise, I read in the bible that some of the battles of ancient Israel were not battles at all. So why have You stopped moving in power? When are You as Almighty God going to repeat the events that took place during the reign of King Jehoshaphat? When the Moabites and Ammonites challenged Judah in battle all Jehoshaphat and Your people did was offer praise and worship to Your holy name; not a single sword was raised. Did You not grant victory? Why should we have to fight war after war?

So far two world wars have been fought, and some on-going conflicts have world war potential. Now would be a good time to move and destroy all these weapons of war. Better still, You could confiscate the knowledge that leads to the manufacture of such weapons of destruction. Why can't it be prayer and praise from the four corners of the earth? Personally, I prefer praise to the sound of machine guns and bombs!

Well, Holy Trinity, these are just some of the thoughts in the mind of your humble daughter and servant who loves You very much.

Heavenly Father looked at Lord Jesus; and they both looked at Holy Spirit and spoke with one voice…

HOLY TRINITY: I thought she said she was going to praise Us?

LORD JESUS: I am amazed at her boldness and audacity. So much has changed since I left the earth!

A Note of Warning

My dear fellow residents of Upside Down, this is not the way to praise Heavenly Father, Lord Jesus and Holy Spirit. Please, whatever you do, do not copy my bad example. The words in bold are some of the attributes of the Holy Trinity that you can use to offer up pure, heartfelt praise! (*For a more comprehensive list of these attributes please see Appendix I*).

April 4
FRUIT OF THE SPIRIT

DEBBIE: Holy Spirit, are You sitting comfortably on Your throne?

HOLY SPIRIT: Yes I am Debbie, or should I stand?

DEBBIE: No, not really. I just want to have a quiet word with You.

HOLY SPIRIT: Judging from past experience, I better alert the rest of heaven to listen.

After a brief pause...

HOLY SPIRIT: OK Debbie you may proceed.

DEBBIE: Well, Holy Spirit, You know those Your fruit mentioned in the book of Galatians chapter 5?

HOLY SPIRIT: You mean My fruit of **love, joy, peace, longsuffering, kindness, goodness, faithfulness, gentleness, self-control**?

DEBBIE: Yes. Well, I have reservations about bearing some of them.

Holy Spirit looked at me in amazement then spoke gingerly...

HOLY SPIRIT: Which ones in particular?

DEBBIE: Well, let me start from the beginning. I will gladly bear the fruits of **love, joy** and **kindness**. After all being kind never harmed anyone, and I could do with more love and joy in my life. However, I do not want to bear the fruit of **patience** because I have discerned that, should I bear this fruit, Heavenly Father will ask me to be patient in my trials and tribulations. Who wants to be patient when going through difficult times? All I want is an instant solution to my situation!

As for the fruit of **self-control**, let's face it, I do not want to end up as a doormat each time I am provoked. Should I bear this fruit, I know the Lord Jesus will always ask me to turn the other cheek! Quite frankly, I only have two cheeks and I have no intention of having them slapped until they turn blue or purple, or any other colour of the rainbow! Losing your cool and forgetting about self-control from time to time is not such a bad thing is it? As for the fruit of **goodness**; well, I intend to be good only to those who are good to me. Why should I waste my energy on being good to selfish and difficult people?

I will willingly bear the fruit of **peace** as we could all do with a lot more peace on earth.

HOLY SPIRIT: Have you finished your sermon or am I interrupting you?

I could feel Holy Spirit looking sternly down at me.

DEBBIE: I have finished.

Holy Spirit turned to Heavenly Father…

HOLY SPIRIT: Heavenly Father, have You heard the fleshly ideas Your daughter has come up with?

HEAVENLY FATHER: Yes, I heard her. It baffles me where she gets her ideas from. Maybe We should ask her Saviour.

Lord Jesus quickly responded...

LORD JESUS: It has absolutely nothing to do with My holy person. Her doctrines are very earthly and it would appear that she either has not read My sermon on the mount or she simply did not understand it.

HEAVENLY FATHER: It could be that the Sermon on the Mount is missing from her many bibles and, as You know, Debbie has her own version of everything!

Anyway, Holy Spirit, You are her Teacher; what do You intend to do about it?

Holy Spirit sighed and shook His holy head.

HOLY SPIRIT: Not to worry Heavenly Father, I have My way of dealing with pupils like Debbie. Please roll out Your pruning shears and prepare to prune her.

When I heard the word 'prune', I almost had a heart attack. Fear and panic gripped me. (For those of you in Upside Down who do not know the implications, I can tell you for free Heavenly Father's pruning shears are very, very sharp, and when He prunes you will feel it. The last time He pruned me I did not enjoy it one bit and swore that it would never happen to me again. In fact I live in terror of Heavenly Father's shears).

Heavenly Father knew He had me in the one spot I dread the most. He left me to silently meditate on whether I wanted to be pruned or, of my own free will, agree to bear ALL the fruit of the Holy Spirit. In the end I chose the smart option.

DEBBIE: Once again I repent. I am sorry and I promise to bear ALL the fruit of Holy Spirit.

LORD JESUS: I must congratulate You Holy Spirit on Your excellent approach. You allow Debbie and her brothers and sisters to come up with their earthly and fleshly ideas then proceed to teach otherwise.

The angels and saints in heaven thanked the Holy Spirit and resumed praise.

You cannot claim to be a Spirit-filled Christian without bearing the fruit of the Holy Spirit.

May 6
PURGATORY?

DEBBIE: Lord Jesus, do You have time for a friendly chat?

LORD JESUS: Is all well Debbie, or do I need to sit on the edge of my throne?

DEBBIE: *Haba!*[3] Lord Jesus, I only need some clarification.

LORD JESUS: OK, proceed.

DEBBIE: Where on earth, heaven or hell is Purgatory?

Lord Jesus looked alarmed.

LORD JESUS: Is this something I taught while I was on earth?

DEBBIE: Well, I do not recall it being mentioned in the bible but I have heard about it.

LORD JESUS: From whom did you hear of it?

DEBBIE: From some of my fellow Christian brothers and sisters.

Heavenly Father became interested in this on-going conversation.

HEAVENLY FATHER: This calls for a close examination.

LORD JESUS: Debbie, what exactly happens in Purgatory?

DEBBIE: Going by what I heard, and the little I have read, Purgatory is a place where the souls of believers who died in a state of grace go to be purified of their grave sins before proceeding to heaven. It is like a final purification rite for the soul to achieve the required holiness that would prepare it for eternal life in heaven.

HEAVENLY FATHER: Now, this is getting very interesting. Holy Spirit, what have You been teaching Debbie, and her brothers and sisters?

HOLY SPIRIT: Aw! Heavenly Father how can You ask Me such a question? You know I only teach them the truth. The problem is that many of Debbie's Christian brothers and sisters do not strictly follow My curriculum and end up devising their own. I personally know nothing about Purgatory!

Heavenly Father put on His fatherly tone.

HEAVENLY FATHER: Debbie, you have raised an interesting issue. Do you know of anyone stranded in this Purgatory, or do you know someone who has crossed over from there to heaven so we can ask this person or soul what goes on there?

DEBBIE: How am I supposed to know? Is heaven not under Your management?

HEAVENLY FATHER: Well it is, but even I do not know the location of Purgatory. Tell me a little bit more about it. Who supervises what goes on there, and who decides when a soul is deemed purified enough to proceed to heaven? And by the way, what exactly is a grave sin?

DEBBIE: Heavenly Father, I have told Lord Jesus all I know. However, I have heard that while these poor souls are stranded in Purgatory, the saints on earth help them along their way by offering prayers for them. These saints also help by giving alms, indulgences and works of penance. In short, they do good works on their behalf. I guess the aim is to ensure that these souls do not stay too long in Purgatory, since it is only meant to be a minor detour on their journey to heaven.

LORD JESUS: So Debbie, what happens if the loved ones of those stranded in Purgatory do not do the necessary good works? Do these souls end up in heaven or hell, or do they languish in Purgatory forever?

DEBBIE: I don't know. I suppose You will have to save them from their misery. I must however confess, Heavenly Father, that this concept of Purgatory does not do Your holy reputation any favours. If having believed while on earth that Jesus died and paid for all our sins at Calvary, then the idea of ending up in Purgatory after death to be purified of sins which have already been forgiven really does not add up.

Heavenly Father gave me a piercing look of reproach; the kind of look you get from the head teacher when you have been summoned to his office for being really naughty; a look that seemed to pierce right through my soul! I quaked with fear and terror and said to myself, "I am guilty as charged, whatever it is that I have done wrong". He then said sternly...

HEAVENLY FATHER: I know Holy Spirit did not teach you about Purgatory neither did Jesus, and I did not reveal this to you in My Holy textbook, the bible. So, stick strictly to the Holy Spirit's curriculum and stop giving Me a holy headache with your non-existent Purgatory! Case dismissed!

There was a sigh of relief in heaven and once again all the angels and saints resumed praise. As usual, I wished with all my heart that I had not started this conversation in the first place.

Do not be deceived and pin your hope on Purgatory as there is no such place. Learn to confess your sins regularly and ask your Heavenly Father for forgiveness.

May 11
THE NAME CHANGE

DEBBIE: Heavenly Father!

HEAVENLY FATHER: Yes Debbie, I hope I have not done anything to upset the residents of Upside Down?

DEBBIE: Eh, Heavenly Father You are OK; You are pure and holy and very unlikely to break any of my unwritten Upside Down rules, commandments, doctrines or religious practices.

Heavenly Father heaved a sigh of relief.

HEAVENLY FATHER: That is a relief! At least I can sit comfortably on My throne. So, what can I do for you my daughter?

DEBBIE: Well, I am finding it difficult to keep saying Heavenly Father each time I want to talk to You, especially in Upside Down language.

Heavenly Father looked perplexed.

HEAVENLY FATHER: So, what do you suggest Debbie?

DEBBIE: I have come up with a solution. From now on is it OK if I just call You HF, i.e. Your initials?

Heavenly Father was silent as He was amazed at my temerity. The angels and saints in heaven were horrified. But the Lord Jesus and the Holy Spirit were on hand to step in before this conversation between Father and daughter got out of hand.

LORD JESUS: Well Heavenly Father, look on the bright side; it may not be such a bad idea. After all You are known as Yahweh, Jehovah, God; Your list of names is endless and one more name should not do any harm.

HOLY SPIRIT: You never know, HF might do wonders for You.

Heavenly Father took heart, gave me a look of exasperation and then, in a stern fatherly voice:

HEAVENLY FATHER: OK Debbie, but only as long as you make it clear what it stands for.

DEBBIE: Thank You HF.

HEAVENLY FATHER: So what about Jesus and Holy Spirit? Do they become LJ and HS?

I whispered hesitantly...

DEBBIE: They remain the same!

HEAVENLY FATHER: Aha, *abajo*⁴, you change My name to HF but the names of your Saviour and Teacher remain the same *abi*⁵?

Lord Jesus and the Holy Spirit smiled.

LORD JESUS: What seems to be the problem here? I see that the girl has done it again! She has come up with an upside down, common sense approach. I like your style Debbie! Maybe there is such a thing as the gift of imagination after all. By the way, Heavenly Father, I do like Your new name!

HOLY SPIRIT: So do I.

After a pause that seemed to go on for eternity...

HEAVENLY FATHER: OK, I will make this exception for the inhabitants of Upside Down.

And so it was that my Heavenly Father blessed His new name and the saints and angels could not help but marvel at this interesting turn of events.

Note of Warning

Fellow residents of Upside Down, please DO NOT go to a Christian gathering and start saying, "My HF, who art in heaven". Neither should you say something like, "I pronounce a blessing in the name of HF, Lord Jesus and Holy Spirit. If you do I can guarantee you will receive fatherly rebuke from Heavenly Father, and a look of reproach from Lord Jesus and Holy Spirit.

MY RELIGION

DEBBIE: Holy Spirit, can I ask You for a big favour?

HOLY SPIRIT: Yes Debbie, go ahead. What do you want?

DEBBIE: I want You to give me one or two earth-shattering, and very profound revelations, dreams or visions that will change the world forever.

HOLY SPIRIT: Debbie, please wait a minute

Holy Spirit looked at Heavenly Father and Lord Jesus.

HOLY SPIRIT: Have You heard the latest from Debbie?

HF: Indeed I have.

He turned His attention to Debbie

HF: So Debbie, what will you do with this profound revelation?

I was silently meditating on how best to break the news to Holy Trinity. I was also thinking about what Lord Jesus would make of my answer. So, in a whisper, silently hoping they would not hear...

DEBBIE: I am thinking of starting my own religion!

As soon as I said it, the angels and saints in heaven stopped praise and worship and started interceding on my behalf. They knew that something was not quite right.

HF: Jesus, did You just hear what I heard?

LORD JESUS: Yes HF, I heard. Actually, I almost fell off My throne.

Holy Spirit decided to continue the conversation...

HOLY SPIRIT: So, why do you want to start your own religion? Is the Christian faith not enough for you?

DEBBIE: Well Holy Spirit, if You can give revelation to the founders of the Jehovah's Witnesses, the Church of Scientology, the Mormons, the Rosicrucian Order, the Grail Message, Eckankar and all these other religions is it not time You evened the score by giving revelation to a woman so she can start her own religion? After all we live in an equal opportunity society yet so far no woman has started a world-wide religion.

HOLY SPIRIT: What makes you think that I give revelation to start new religions?

DEBBIE: Well, that is the impression given; that all revelation to start new religions comes from You or an angel.

LORD JESUS: So Debbie, who will be the head of this new religion?

DEBBIE: Ah, um, well, there will still be a place for You as a mighty prophet of God, but I suppose, it would only be right for me to be the head of my own religion – I will be the main guru!

LORD JESUS: So you no longer need a saviour do you?

DEBBIE: I guess You could say that. I will be in charge and the religion will deliver us! That is the whole point.

LORD JESUS: So where do you intend to get the doctrine for your new religion from?

DEBBIE: That should not be too difficult as most of it already exists in the various religions of the world. In addition to the revelation the Holy Spirit gives me, I will find a verse or passage in the bible that I will interpret to suit my purpose. After all, that is what some of these other religions seem to do. A case in point would be the Jehovah's Witnesses and Isaiah 43:10. Talk about interpreting the bible the wrong way round and upside down!

I will borrow a bit from the Scientology manual; and pick out some choice bits from the Hindu, Shinto, Buddhism and Hare Krishna faiths. Then to crown it all, I will add a sprinkling of authentic African religion on ancestral worship, and mix that with some New Age teaching.

The doctrines of my religion will be explicitly and perfectly written. I tell You Lord Jesus, my religion will be one of the wonders of the world as I will use everything the Holy Spirit has taught me, and add a few of my own ideas. Followers of my religion will also be well grounded in my interpretation of world philosophies, such as Humanism.

HOLY SPIRIT: So Debbie, where do I fit into this new religion of yours?

DEBBIE: Once You have given me the profound revelation, Your services will no longer be required. I will take on the role of teacher, counsellor and comforter. However there will be an everlasting memorial and reference to You as the source of my revelation.

HF: Will I have a role to play in your religion, or have I also been made redundant?

Debbie: *Ewo*[6], HF! How can I have a religion without You? Of course, there is a role for You. However Your job description will need to be amended. You will be a Supreme Being, out there and far away, generally supervising everything and occasionally getting involved in the affairs of mankind when I invite You.

At this point the angels and saints in heaven intensified their intercession. Even some saints on earth joined them fearing that this could be the end of Debbie.

Holy Spirit: So, let Me get this right. This new religion of yours does not need a Saviour; you have made it quite clear that you will not need Me, and HF is more or less made redundant right? Where will you take the followers of your religion after death?

I was silent.

Debbie: Maybe we will *astralise*[7] to the planet Neptune or Jupiter and colonise it.

HF: And what makes you think that you will have control over your soul after death?

More prolonged silence.

Holy Spirit: Have you heard that there is such a thing as negative revelation given by the enemy gang leader, Satan?

Interestingly I had not thought about this and I was forced into serious meditation.

Lord Jesus: Has it occurred to you that I just might cast you and your followers into hell and eternal damnation?

It was becoming more obvious by the second that once again I had not thought this through. My meditation went into overdrive. Right then Heavenly Father looked at Lord Jesus and Holy Spirit…

HF: Never mind, Debbie and the followers of her religion will face Me after death, and they will feel the full force of My wrath. On that day they will know that divine judgement is not a figment of man's imagination.

Terror gripped my heart; I was beginning to drown in my own sweat. I entered a period of deep reflection. I knew I had made a grave mistake.

Knowing that there was nothing that Heavenly Father could not do, I did not want Him to implement His threat earlier than expected. I fell to my knees and repented in dust and ashes before Him. I then went on to address the residents of Upside Down:

DEBBIE: Hang on folks; all plans to start my own religion have been shelved as I do not relish the prospect of spending eternity in hell. I am really, really sorry for misleading you!

LORD JESUS: I see that you have come to your senses!

✦

"There is a way that seems right to a man, but its end is the way of death." (Proverbs 14:12)

May 23
FOR THE SAKE OF ONE

DEBBIE: Lord Jesus, can I point something out to You?

LORD JESUS: Wait a minute; let Me gather the whole of heaven to listen to what you have to say this time around.

Lord Jesus summoned all of heaven to listen, and once again fixed His gaze on me...

LORD JESUS: Go ahead Debbie.

DEBBIE: For some reason I do not get the point of the Parable of the Lost Sheep. In my mind it seems like You failed to understand the principles of accounting; You let Your emotions get the better of You.

Lord Jesus, have You not heard of profit and loss? Ninety nine sheep were already safe yet You risked their lives to pursue the life of one lost sheep. It just does not make sense. In any part of the world, if you score 99% in an exam, you will be awarded an A***. So, why bother with one stray sheep when You have already done outstandingly well? A 1% loss in most businesses is considered negligible anyway.

Lord Jesus looked at me with compassion and spoke in a soft voice...

LORD JESUS: Debbie, do you remember the time when you were that one lost sheep? How would you have felt if I had left you to go astray without seeking you out?

Suddenly it all made sense to me.

DEBBIE: Thank You Lord Jesus for risking the ninety nine safe Christians just to rescue me.

———⌒~~~⌒———

"I say to you that likewise there will be more joy in heaven over one sinner who repents than over ninety-nine just persons who need no repentance." (Luke 15:7) If you are that one lost sheep, start making your way to Jesus. Your Heavenly Father is waiting with outstretched arms ready to receive you into the fold.

June 7
REINCARNATION OR RESURRECTION

DEBBIE: Holy Spirit, do You mind if I ask You a question?

HOLY SPIRIT: Of course not; please go ahead.

DEBBIE: What is the difference between resurrection and reincarnation?

Holy Spirit turned to Heavenly Father and Lord Jesus, as if to say, "Here we go again". I on the other hand found it hard to understand why my Teacher had to get Heavenly Father and Lord Jesus involved; all I did was ask a simple question!

LORD JESUS: Debbie, are you trying to say that after all these years of being a Christian; spending hours listening to sermons, plus one to one tuition and tutorials with the Holy Spirit, as well as divine input from HF and Myself, you still do not know what the resurrection is?

DEBBIE: Well, I thought I knew until a friend confused me.

Heavenly Father shook His head; disappointment written all over His face.

HF: Disgrace upon disgrace! So Debbie, what is reincarnation, and is it part of the Christian faith?

DEBBIE: Well, as far as I know, it is not part of the Christian faith but I was hoping Holy Spirit would shed more light on this.

HOLY SPIRIT: Normally I stick strictly to My Curriculum and the holy textbook – the bible, but in this instance I will make an exception.

Debbie, have you done any research on reincarnation and what it means?

I was beginning to regret asking this question as I was now being forced to research things outside the Christian faith. This will teach me to keep my big mouth shut.

DEBBIE: Reincarnation is a complex minefield that has a theology of its own, but I will try my best to explain my findings.

HOLY SPIRIT: All I require is a simple explanation so that the residents of Upside Down can understand it.

DEBBIE: Ok, I will try and keep it simple. So, here goes:

Reincarnation is a kind of recycling of the soul; a continuous rebirth of the soul in another body after death. This may not necessarily be in another human body as a soul could reincarnate as an animal, or even a vegetable.

In some religions reincarnation is regarded as a bad thing as it means the soul has not yet been perfected. In some others, it is viewed as a reward or punishment for good or evil done in a previous life. Thus, the good or ill-fortune a person may be experiencing in their present life is a direct reward or punishment for something they did in a previous life.

However, there are other religions that believe reincarnation is a good thing as it gives one the chance to put right the wrong they did in a previous life.

In a nutshell, it seems that all the religions that do believe in reincarnation have varying concepts of what it means.

So, after my research I am none the wiser as I am still left with many unanswered questions; questions such as, "Since no one reincarnates as themselves, how does the reincarnated person know the right or wrong they did in a previous life?" Or, "If one reincarnates as a vegetable or vice versa, how would it know how it lived in the life before?"

Holy Spirit: Now that you seem to have grasped the main gist of reincarnation, can you explain, in simple terms, your understanding of resurrection?

Debbie: Resurrection is the bodily rising from the dead; like what happened to Jesus on the very first Easter. The souls of all who have died will be resurrected on the last day, when Christ shall return in His second coming to reign on earth. The souls of those who placed their faith in Christ as their Lord and Saviour will be resurrected to everlasting life while the souls of those who rejected Him will resurrect to eternal damnation. All souls will be resurrected to face divine judgement!

Resurrection is a onetime occurrence. The soul does not get stuck in an endless cycle of being reborn in another person, or animate object. I believe you resurrect as yourself and you will meet and recognise friends and loved ones who have also died. For believers, it is definitely a happy re-union.

Holy Spirit: Which do you prefer Debbie – reincarnation or resurrection?

Debbie: Now what kind of question is that? Of course I prefer resurrection, and I look forward to coming back as myself! What rest is there from my labours if I spend eternity reincarnating as someone or something else?

And what if my soul is not perfected, where will I end up and how many lives must I live to achieve perfection? Anyway, the thought of reincarnating as an ant or a carrot is not exactly appealing.

Jesus is the resurrection and the life, NOT the reincarnation.

June 10
MOTHER OF GOD

LORD JESUS: Debbie!

I was alarmed!

DEBBIE: Yes Lord Jesus

LORD JESUS: I want you to do Me a big favour.

DEBBIE: Should it not be the other way round? I mean, what favour could I possibly do for You?

LORD JESUS: You will soon find out. The thing is, all this whispering in My ear is doing My head in, as they say in England. So do you think you could educate the residents of Upside Down about this practice?

DEBBIE: Lord Jesus, who is whispering in Your ear? From my limited experience of Pentecostal and Charismatic churches, I would have thought that shouting, not whispering, was the issue!

HOLY SPIRIT: Debbie, My dear pupil, once again you disgrace Me your Teacher. Are you so dim? Have you not heard that some of your brothers and sisters ask the Virgin Mary to whisper their petitions to Jesus?

HF: A bit surprising; she is usually as sharp as a razor, when it suits her!

DEBBIE: Oh, now I get it. But I would not want to provoke fire and brimstone to stream down Mount Vatican to consume me. As You know Holy Trinity is unseen, and I do not know if I can take the heat. Now that You mention it, isn't holy Mary Your earthly mother; mother of God; queen of heaven and all that? What is wrong with her whispering a few petitions in Your ear? It is quite possible that those who believe in such prayers get their results a lot quicker than the rest of us! In fact, I am tempted to try this approach myself.

HOLY SPIRIT: If you try that approach I will teach you a lesson you will never forget. The key question for you and mankind is, "Who did you see hanging on the cross at Calvary; was it the mother of God?"

DEBBIE: Ah, no! Only the Lord Jesus gave His life on the cross at Calvary. But hold on a minute; I thought I was supposed to be doing Lord Jesus a favour here.

HOLY SPIRIT: So now you think you can hold Us to ransom do you? Nice try! Now get on with the assignment you have been given and stop all this nonsense!

HF: To update you; the problem is not only with the whispering, but also the way this is slowly, but surely, taking away from the person and work of Jesus. Remember, it is written, *"My glory I will not give to another"*[8]. There are even prayers in her name and when these Christians pray, they believe that it is holy Mary granting their petitions instead of Me.

There are thousands of shrines in her honour and visions of the Virgin Mary are being seen all around the world. Those who claim to have seen and received instructions from her have not even bothered to question the source of these visions and the number of those seeking apparitions of her is on the increase. Look Debbie, there is a whole theology about the Virgin Mary and I find the whole thing quite displeasing.

Holy Spirit: And to add to that, it is beginning to look like the Virgin Mary has become the fourth person of Holy Trinity.

Debbie: My fellow Upside Down residents, you can see the seriousness of this matter. For those of you who believe in Virgin Mary, I hate to disappoint you because she has no more access to Jesus than you and I. In fact, she is dead and neither needs, nor can she give, access to Christ. And for the record, HF has not given her the power or authority to answer prayers!

Her mission is completed and her everlasting blessing is indeed great for she is foremost amongst women. In fact the story of the gospel and the salvation that God wrought for man cannot be told without reference to her obedience. However, let us not get carried away, she like the rest of us, is a servant of Almighty God. For those of you who take things a bit too far, can you answer the question the Holy Spirit asked; "Who gave His life for you on the cross at Calvary?"

Well, before now you could argue that you were misled but this is no longer an excuse. Anyone or anything that exalts itself above Christ will be brought down. Lord Jesus will not share His glory or praise with anyone, it does not matter who they are.

Out of curiosity, having singled out Virgin Mary, what about Joseph? Did he not play a part as well? How come he is not called step-father of God?

DEBBIE: But Lord Jesus, why have You waited hundreds of years to do something about this? Why was this not nipped in the bud? Is this not like the fall of man repeating itself? I mean, HF could have stopped this there in the Garden of Eden but chose to allow it and we had to wait thousands of years to be reconciled with Him.

LORD JESUS: Let Us just say that your write up is one in a long list of warnings given by My prophets before I take final action. Remember, I have all eternity to achieve My purpose but My patience is wearing thin and I can assure you that it will not go on forever.

HF: The day is soon coming when I will order My angels to remove all images of Virgin Mary, and other vexatious images and objects from My house. Then the world will know just how displeased I have been.

Archangel Gabriel murmurs to himself...

ARCHANGEL GABRIEL: Sometimes the girl talks sense! Mother of God, step-father of God, queen of heaven hmm! These humans really know how to wear out God's patience and exalt a person in a way God has not chosen. What I would really like to know is where they get their theology from, and who puts these ideas in their heads!

Virgin Mary, the mother of Jesus, is an example to us all of humility and obedience to God. However, this does not mean that we should weave a theology around her, or ascribe attributes to her that HF has not given.

June 12
FEAR NOT, I AM WITH YOU

Being the busybody that I am, I decided to call a meeting of all the residents of Upside Down country:

DEBBIE: My fellow residents of Upside Down have you noticed a curious pattern in the bible? HF hardly ever chooses the brave people of this world. For some reason He seems to go for those who are reluctant to carry out His missions; a reluctance that is usually backed up with good reasons. He also often sends people on dangerous missions and assignments.

Take Moses for instance, he was an unlikely leader - a stammerer who fled Egypt after committing murder. Then God stepped in and sent him back to confront Pharaoh. Would anyone in their right mind accept that assignment?

Then there was Gideon. He was the one that the angel called a *mighty man of valour*. Now, here was a man who was so fearful of the Midianite oppressors that he threshed wheat in a winepress. Then God comes along and sends him, with just three hundred men, into battle against an army; an enemy "as numerous as locusts; with camels too numerous to count, as many as the sand on the seashore in multitude".

The trend continues with the prophet Samuel when he was sent by God to anoint David as king, whilst Saul was still on the throne of Israel. As one would expect, Samuel was fearful for his life, and if you think this was an easy task then think again! Just put yourself in Samuel's shoes; how would you have felt if God sent you to anoint someone as the next president of Uganda while Idi Amin was still president? You can be sure that if your actions came to light, you were as good as dead!

Also, we should not forget Elijah, when he faced King Ahab of Israel. Can you imagine an audience with the Prime Minister of Great Britain and you proclaim a three year drought because the nation had sinned and turned its back on God? I do not need to tell you that when the drought kicks in your life would no longer be worth living. You would be accused of every crime under the sun, including the practice of witchcraft and voodoo.

And of course there was the case of the prophet Nathan with King David. Would you be brave enough to confront the President of the United States of America and accuse him of adultery and murder?

We have to raise our hats to these brave men of Almighty God. However, the time has come for God to change His tactics and we have to find a way to convince Him. Let's face it, if you are a real chicken like me, how would you confront the powerful people of this world; the modern day Pharaohs of our generation?

Many Upside Down residents agreed with me and one even suggested that we write a petition to persuade Almighty God to change His ways. I had not invited any person of the Trinity to this gathering as it was not a prayer meeting but suddenly, out of nowhere, like a whirlwind, Lord Jesus showed up.

LORD JESUS: Look at them; a group of cowards who call themselves Christians; a people who will not do or say anything to exalt God. And you Debbie, the ring leader, tell Me, out of all the those you mentioned earlier, how many of them failed to accomplish the purpose of God? Did He not say, "His presence will go with them?" As for these so-called modern day Pharaohs, who created them? Who gives them breath in their nostrils? Have I not said that "*My strength is made perfect in weakness?[9]*"

Once again I was rendered speechless.

"But the cowardly...shall have their part in the lake which burns with fire and brimstone, which is the second death" (Revelation 21:8)

June 14
LOST BUT FOUND

The story of my life so far according to Holy Trinity.

HF: Debbie, are you awake and sitting comfortably?

Why was Heavenly Father calling me? I was panic stricken. My heart was beating at an extremely fast pace as I answered...

DEBBIE: What's wrong HF? Why are You calling me? Aren't I the one who always calls You?

HOLY SPIRIT: Aha! That used to be the case but We have decided to turn the tables on you. We want to tell you a story. It just might sound familiar, so brace yourself.

I was anxious at this turn of events, but I managed to keep silent.

LORD JESUS: The story is about a girl. It all started in 1958 when this girl's father, a nice Christian man, prayed and asked God for a daughter as his first born child. The angels could not decide which person of Holy Trinity put the idea in his head but they could see that it pleased Almighty God greatly, and at that time HF commented about the girl's father, *"He must have read My mind; definitely a man after My own heart."* Well, this girl was duly born in 1959 into a Christian family.

HOLY SPIRIT: At the time of her birth the whole of heaven rejoiced and Holy Trinity pronounced blessings over her. HF, leading the way, decided that she would be an Anglican.

LORD JESUS: HF, are You sure about this? She has been born into a Baptist family.

HF: Never You mind, she will be an Anglican.

LORD JESUS: I am not completely satisfied. If she must be an Anglican, I want her to be a Charismatic Anglican.

HOLY SPIRIT: Personally I want her to be a Pentecostal, Evangelical Anglican.

HF: If there is still space, I want her to be a conservative, orthodox Anglican.

LORD JESUS: HF what is that?

HF: You tell Me; here I was thinking that they were all supposed to be just Christians.

Altogether, Holy Trinity pronounced that she would be a Pentecostal, Charismatic Evangelical, Conservative, Orthodox Anglican! The angels were horrified but kept silent.

HF: As expected, the girl was brought up in the church but even at this early stage of her life, she showed that she had a tendency to stray off course, much to My chagrin.

The first minor hiccup to My plan occurred while she was in primary school. At the grand age of seven she decided that she wanted to be a Catholic. Jesus was sent to rescue the mission and she was promptly despatched to an Anglican primary school. She also began to attend an Anglican Church. The rest of her primary school education was uneventful.

LORD JESUS: HF did not take any more chances. He took personal charge and made sure that she was sent to an

Anglican secondary boarding school. This was to ensure the good work that had been started in primary school would continue and she would be grounded in the doctrines and ways of worship of the church. While there, Holy Spirit urged her to join the Christian fellowship. She attended one prayer meeting; she liked the singing but could not abide by the dress code and their religious practices.

HF: I was alarmed as I could see she was slipping away from Me. Holy Spirit assured Me that all was not lost as she was taking part in the religious life of the school. However I had My doubts as she refused to be baptised. So, once again I took matters into My own hands and when she was fourteen years old I spoke to her directly and asked if she would like to be a *Moses*? Fortunately, she said, "Yes".

HOLY SPIRIT: There was a sigh of relief in heaven and We felt this was a promising new beginning. So, off she went to university to finish off her education. We had misgivings about this as, left to Us, she should have been sent to a Theology College to train for ministry. However, her father persuaded Us and besides, she was nowhere ready for life in ministry.

LORD JESUS: We were proved right. Once again at the prompting of Holy Spirit, she attempted to join the Christian fellowship. She went to their services a few times but was thoroughly put off, and the allure of the world proved just too strong for her to resist.

Before We knew it she was completely lost in the world. She forgot Almighty God, her Creator. HF lamented bitterly, and predictably I was despatched on a rescue mission; this time to save HF from going into depression.

HOLY SPIRIT: The mission was a success all thanks to Jesus. HF came up with a plan that would make sure she married a nice Anglican man. We all agreed and approved of this, but her earthly father threatened to derail this divine arrangement. However, he was no match for HF. HF promptly arranged for her mother-in-law to have her baptised in the Anglican Church, in accordance with His will.

HF: She settled down well and her marriage blossomed. She made a decision to take her faith seriously, something she backed up by attending church regularly. For once, My heart was glad as it was an Anglican church. But then trials and tribulations struck. This made her husband see the light and he gave his life to Jesus; he became born again. Her husband then tried to persuade and encourage her to do likewise.

LORD JESUS: "Born again", she screamed, "What for? I have been a Christian all my life, why do I need to be born again?"

HF: I looked at Holy Spirit and asked, "As an authority in this matter, what is her position?"

HOLY SPIRIT: Well, technically she is right. She does not need to be born again for the umpteenth time. She is a Christian and that really is the end of the matter.

Heavenly Father breathed a sigh of relief.

LORD JESUS: To continue the story, she took her faith seriously. She began to read her bible and attended a few religious gatherings, and evangelistic crusades.

She remained in the faith but not in the way Holy Spirit wanted.

She began to show signs of wandering off again. Her excuse this time was that she was bored with the way Anglican services were conducted. In her own words, "They were nothing but boring repetitions of the collect".

HOLY SPIRIT: Not satisfied with the little progress on the faith front, HF, in His infinite wisdom, decided to uproot her to England without her prior knowledge. Both Lord Jesus and Myself were alarmed but we went along with HF. In fact, she nearly derailed the plan when she bluntly refused to emigrate. But HF has His ways. He despatched her husband to make sure that His emigration plan succeeded.

HF: She arrived in England with her family but made up her mind that she would never again step into an Anglican church. Meanwhile, I had taken the trouble to ensure that there was a Charismatic Church of England church on her doorstep.

Armed with a list of all the local churches, she proceeded to spend her first year in England trying out various Pentecostal and Charismatic churches. Well, I will not go into detail of her experience in these churches because that is another matter but it was not exactly pleasant. I was left with no choice but to wring my hands in despair and hope that she would come to her senses.

In the end I had to appeal to Holy Spirit to re-direct her to the Church of England. Strangely enough, she co-operated with the proviso that it was a temporary move to stop her from backsliding and she would only stay there until she found a church of her liking.

Lord Jesus: HF wasted no time; He promptly made sure she was confirmed in the Church of England. At last, she began to grow in faith in a way that pleased Holy Trinity and once again heaven breathed a sigh of relief.

Holy Spirit: How the next phase in her development happened is simply a mystery. There We were watching her growth with pride and joy when suddenly she started flirting with Trade Unionism with a zeal that amazed Us. We had to move quickly. HF promptly asked Jesus to embark on another rescue mission. The mission was accomplished when, after a sharp rebuke from HF, she came to her senses. She went back to concentrating her energy in the church and once again began to follow the curriculum I had designed for her.

Lord Jesus: Just when We thought all was plain sailing, disaster struck. This was the worst she had suffered so far. The unthinkable happened right under Our very noses; she got lost in the muddy waters of religion with a zeal that would have put Paul, before his conversion, to shame. I am certain that neither the Pharisees nor the Sadducees could match her fervour. There she was practicing all the 'dos' and 'don'ts' which HF had not commanded; things that were unnecessary under the terms of the new covenant.

Space will not permit Me to give the detailed account of her journey into religion, which she went on under the misguided belief that she was pleasing her Heavenly Father. She could write a manual for religious people from her own experience alone. So, maybe you can now see where the idea to start her own religion came from.

HF: I was heartbroken. I could not understand why she had to stray into the muddy waters of religion. Why now when everything was going so well? I do not even know if she was following Old or New Testament religion! This was definitely a job for Jesus; yet another rescue mission!

LORD JESUS: I could not help but ask Myself, "How many rescue missions must I do for one person?" There had to be a limit. I hoped this would be the last time but something inside Me knew that there would be more.

Holy Spirit did not waste any time to confirm what Lord Jesus was thinking.

HOLY SPIRIT: I won't bet on it, knowing her, she is more likely to stray into something else.

Anyway with great difficulty and the special effort of Holy Trinity, Lord Jesus brought her home on His shoulder; mud and all. HF was overjoyed; He brought out the whitest of towels and cleaned the mud off her. Even the angels could not help protesting at this lavish waste of such a white towel.

After cleaning her, He put on her His very best royal robe; just like the one He was wearing, only smaller. He then ordered a banquet for her, and the whole of heaven rejoiced.

LORD JESUS: Well, the story did not end there. She was very repentant when HF pointed out to her what she had done wrong, especially when she realised that He was not impressed with her efforts. If anything, He hated the whole sorry episode. Holy Spirit sternly made her realise that He had deliberately omitted religion from His curriculum and therefore she had acquired this religious knowledge from the world.

HOLY SPIRIT: Jesus, are You keeping a record of all these rescue missions? At the rate she is going, do you think she will find her way to heaven?

LORD JESUS: I have already lost count of the rescue missions and to answer your question, she is more likely to stray into Purgatory and try out whatever religion they practice there before she finds out that she is in the wrong place!

HF: Holy Spirit, now that she is back from the land of religion, We have to do something to stop her from straying. If You do not take control and anoint her as planned, I will not be responsible for what she chooses to stray into next.

LORD JESUS: Holy Spirit took the Fatherly advice. He anointed her and launched her into ministry. The ministry went according to plan and was successful until the flesh reared its ugly head again.

She combined the worst of the flesh with the Spirit. Holy Spirit was horrified! This war between the flesh and the Spirit cannot be documented in this narrative as it may not be beneficial to new Christians.

HF: Holy Spirit was teaching her one thing and she was learning something else. She even strayed into the domain of the enemy, thanks to some of her brothers and sisters. She began to acquire knowledge in demonology and similar topics. Holy Spirit was in despair and was threatening to shut down her classes. But then He had a bright idea.

Meanwhile, in this instance Jesus decided that there would be no rescue mission as the flesh profits Him nothing.

Holy Spirit: Out of despair, I sent an *SOS* to HF to prune her and remove the flesh so that My work would not be in vain. HF duly obliged and this had a modest effect. Alas the enemy was not to be left out of this narrative; the battle with the flesh was far from won.

Lord Jesus: As HF is an authority on disciplining wayward and difficult children, the task fell on Him to sort this out. According to Holy Spirit, HF meditated for one thousandth of a second, even though how He timed it is still a mystery. By the way, this is definitely not the way to meditate. If you intend to follow HF's example, then be prepared to receive a very long lecture from Holy Spirit.

HF looked into His bag of disciplinary tools and came up with the perfect solution: The cup of affliction courtesy of Satan. HF allowed the evil one to afflict her. However, He knew that He would turn it round for good. This plan, though painful, had the backing of Holy Trinity. Holy Spirit and I went into a time of intense intercession so that the trial would not break her.

HF: What an affliction it proved to be as Satan chose one of the worst in his arsenal of afflictions. I cried My heart out just watching her.

Lord Jesus: It took HF seven years to repair the damage done by the evil one, and through it all He carried His daughter. When He felt the time was right, He set her down on her feet and Holy Spirit began to re-educate her in the way of the Spirit.

HF: To everyone's amazement, the flesh was taken care of and all the work of the Evil One was undone. The blessings began to flow! Unbelievably, she surrendered all areas of her life to the Lordship of Jesus and began to walk by the Spirit.

HOLY SPIRIT: I cannot describe the joy in the heart of the Holy Trinity. Best of all, she came to the realisation that she was meant to be an Anglican and embraced her destiny. She fell in love with the collects and the way Anglican services were done. The angels rejoiced, as they had been keenly watching the whole saga. It is still not clear if she is a Charismatic, Pentecostal or Evangelical Anglican; the jury is out on that one. HF may yet get His wish; she could end up a conservative, orthodox Anglican.

LORD JESUS: Holy Spirit, with the backing of HF and Myself, launched her into ministry a second time.

HF: Debbie, are you still listening? You seem to be awfully quiet.

HOLY SPIRIT: She needs to be resuscitated; she has fainted out of embarrassment.

Debbie, listen very carefully. Jesus will not be carrying out any more rescue missions as you have already used up your allotted portion. So think carefully before straying into something else. Besides, HF has made up His mind that His heart can no longer take it.

LORD JESUS: Now is your chance to showcase the excellent teaching that you have received from Holy Spirit; now is the time to make your Teacher proud of you. Your Heavenly Father is also very anxious to show off His daughter to the world. So, as you normally tell Us, put on your best daughterly behaviour and avoid giving Him a holy heart attack.

All the angels and saints in heaven said, "Amen! Go girl".

July 5
NEVER LATE

DEBBIE: HF!

HF: Yes Debbie, I thought I was on a break from you. Now what do you want?

DEBBIE: Well HF, there are certain aspects of Your character we do not like.

HF: Wait a minute.

Heavenly Father looked at Lord Jesus and Holy Spirit and said, "Did You hear that? It seems like Debbie is about to psychoanalyse Me".

HF: Now My dear daughter, which aspects in particular do you have issues with?

DEBBIE: Well, HF, we, that is me and a few other children of Yours, believe that You are sometimes too slow when it comes to answering our prayers. Do You think You could speed things up a bit?

Heavenly Father was silent for a while.

HF: My dear Debbie, how did you arrive at this conclusion?

DEBBIE: HF, how long have You got?

HF: Eternity!

I was temporarily thrown and unsure of how to proceed.

DEBBIE: Ah, um! I do not think what I have to say will take that long.

HF: OK, you may proceed.

DEBBIE: Thank You. I would like to take You on a trip through the bible starting with Adam & Eve.

When Adam & Eve yielded to temptation and fell, You already had it in mind to send the Messiah. Moses spoke about it, David spoke about it, and the prophets prophesied it. But it still took You thousands of years to send the Messiah. As it is, some of us have embraced Christ as our Messiah, while others are still waiting for theirs, and some do not even think they need a Messiah. Perhaps, the second coming of Jesus will convince them but by then it would be a case of *"garri*[10] *don pass water or water don pass garri"*[11]; as we say in Pidgin English. Whichever way you look at it, it would be an unmitigated disaster as the second coming equals the judgment!

Talking about the second coming; we are still waiting for Christ to come again after two millennia. The worrying thing is that the bible says a thousand years are like a day in Your eyes so we could be waiting for a very long time. This is a little hard on some of us who want to experience the rapture.

Then, take a look at Abraham. At the age of seventy five You promised him a son, but he had to wait twenty five years to see that come to pass. I would not exactly call that fast service, would You?

As for David, he was anointed as king while he was a mere youth, but it took a while before he sat on the throne of Israel.

HF: Debbie, have you finished your analysis?

Debbie: I think so.

HF: Exactly how many bibles do you have? And starting with yourself, can you point to any time when your prayers were answered late?

I was silent. I scratched my head and searched the deepest parts of my memory but I could not come up with an instance when Heavenly Father had not answered my prayers on time. I had no choice but to concede that, while God may appear slow to the human mind, He is never late when it comes to answering our prayers. He is always on time.

Holy Spirit caused me to remember a piece of scripture which I had conveniently forgotten: "the Lord is not slow in keeping His promises, as some understand slowness" (2 Peter 3:9a, NIV). Again I found myself repenting in dust and ashes before Heavenly Father took disciplinary action against me. But I guess He knew I would soon be back with another cheeky comment!

God answers ALL prayers according to His own timetable. He is never late with His answers. Just have faith and wait patiently for Him.

July 17
YOUR WILL, NOT MINE

DEBBIE: Holy Spirit!

HOLY SPIRIT: Yes Debbie. Do not tell Me that you have another question to ask or is it another one of your sermons from the desk? Anyway, what can I do for you?

DEBBIE: Well Holy Spirit, we are very happy that You guide us and give us sound counsel that money could never buy. However, Your guidance and counselling methods are way too painful. Allowing us to go through trials and tribulations to build up our character is way too hard on the heart. From my personal experience, it has reduced me to tears so many times and I cannot rule out more tears in the future. This leaves me somewhat baffled; why can't You just lead and guide us to where we need to be?

HOLY SPIRIT: Can you be more specific and give examples to back up your argument?

DEBBIE: How long have You got? And please do not say eternity.

Holy Spirit smiled and nodded.

DEBBIE: Well, it is my firm belief that the School of Guidance and Counselling à la Holy Spirit is way too painful. If in doubt ask Joseph; sold into slavery by his own brothers, thrown into jail for something he did not even do and all because God was preparing him to be the

Prime Minister of Egypt.

How about David; a fugitive for many years, fleeing for his life, not sure whether to remain in Israel or run to Moab and the land of the Philistines, and all because God promised him the throne of Israel! Left to me, I would have been tempted to tell HF to keep the throne of Israel; let me have some peace and sleep on my own bed and not in a cave!

And it is not just in the Old Testament. What about John the Baptist who lost his life because he spoke the truth and was sent to prepare the way for Christ? Or spare a thought for St Paul's sufferings, imprisonments, abandonment by friends, beatings, shipwrecks, persecutions etc., and all because Holy Spirit asked him to be set apart to proclaim the gospel to the Gentiles! He even made the most of St Paul's time in prison by getting him to write some of the epistles. Can you beat that?

I addressed the residents of Upside Down:

Debbie: My fellow citizens of Upside Down, this pattern is not only in the bible as examples abound in history. From what I have discerned, the curriculum for the School of Preparation for Great Blessing is too hard on the heart and mind. Spare a thought for Dr Martin Luther King Jr. who lost his life for standing up for the truth. Is this not a John the Baptist scenario repeating itself in our time? Where would Andrew Young, Jesse Jackson, Colin Powell, Condoleezza Rice and Barack Obama, just to name a few, be without the supreme sacrifice of Martin Luther King Jr.?

Another case in point is Nelson Mandela. From the day his parents rejoiced at his birth, Holy Spirit knew he would one day be the President of South Africa, though He omitted to fill him in on the details! But look at how He guided him through a twenty seven year stint in prison. Are you thinking what I am thinking? Hello! What do prison and president have in common? Is this not a modern day case of Joseph repeating itself? I am sure if you look carefully you too can come up with a few examples of your own.

I turned my attention back to the Holy Spirit...

Holy Spirit, coming back to my main point; I can understand the need to preserve the Davidic lineage based on HF's promises of the Messiah. However, thanks to Lord Jesus, we no longer need a Messiah. As for St Paul, he has accomplished Your mission; where would the Church be without him? Thanks to him, the canon of scripture is complete and there is therefore no need for another St Paul, St Pauline, or St Paula for that matter. What we need now are as many Christians as possible, in every tongue, tribe and nation, to keep the Church ticking along until the second coming of Christ.

As for me, I have decided that I will not be applying for Your course in the School of Preparation for Great Blessing. I also appeal to HF, in the name of Jesus, not to make me any promises, for I have discerned this to be the root of all trials and tribulations. His promises contain hidden dangers which the human mind cannot discern until well after the event.

So, Holy Spirit I beg of You, eternal life in heaven is good enough for me, and since I have already achieved this by faith, Your mission for me is accomplished. Now do not go upsetting the apple cart with promises of superfluous blessings. *Abi na by force*[12]?

Once again I turned to the citizens of Upside Down:

DEBBIE: My dear brothers and sisters, you might want to pray a prayer similar to mine if you wish, but I get the sneaky feeling that this prayer will be like a ball bouncing off a brick wall; Holy Spirit will most likely pay no attention whatsoever. The path our lives will take has already been pre-determined and I do not see Holy Spirit rearranging His plans. So, as usual, I am sorry to disappoint you!

Long after I had forgotten this conversation I felt a tap on my shoulder. It was Holy Spirit…

HOLY SPIRIT: Debbie, My very clever pupil, you have become cleverer than even I your Teacher. It seems you want to teach Me how to change My ways. I who existed before time; I who inhabit eternity; I who was there in the beginning and will be there in the end; I who have thousands of years of experience in counselling and wisely guiding mankind, a feat you will never achieve even if you reincarnated a million times (*assuming that were possible!*). Have you not heard that I, the Lord of hosts, am *"wonderful in counsel and excellent in guidance"*[13]?

Let Me remind you of scriptures you seem to have forgotten. Have you not read in that bible of yours that *"I am the Lord, I do not change"*[14]. Furthermore, have you not read that *"My thoughts are not your thoughts neither are My ways your ways. For as the heavens are higher than the earth, so are My ways higher than your ways and My thoughts, than your thoughts?*[15]

Have you measured the distance between heaven and

earth? What do you have to teach Me who created the universe? Now starting with yourself and going as far back as you want, but preferably to the time of Adam and Eve, give Me one instance when My guidance, counsel, and wisdom failed to achieve My purpose. And the emphasis is **MY PURPOSE!** You may take as long as you like to think about your response.

I was speechless and wished I had not brought this upon myself. This was one assignment I had no intention of doing as I already knew the outcome – Olodo[16], 0%, nil point!

The Holy Spirit does counsel and guide us in ways that are contrary to the ways of this world; ways that are sometimes painful to bear. But be of good cheer for His way is the way of success, personal fulfilment and purpose!

July 17
THE "HOUSEWORK" FAVOUR

DEBBIE: HF!

Heavenly Father sighs.

HF: Yes Debbie.

DEBBIE: I want to ask You for a favour.

HF: OK, wait a minute.

Heavenly Father turns to Lord Jesus and Holy Spirit

HF: Are you listening? It is Debbie again! She wants to ask a favour of Me, and as You both know, I am very wary of her favours. Sometimes I wonder who puts her up to all this!

LORD JESUS: Well HF, she does not need anyone to put ideas in her head for thanks to Holy Spirit, her *gift of imagination* seems to be working overtime.

HOLY SPIRIT: Let Us give the girl a chance; let all of heaven and earth hear what she has to say. You never know, it just might end up in Our favour.

HF: I doubt it very much. When she is not being cheeky or asking awkward questions, she is asking for favours that are often contrary to My will. And of course I have no choice but to listen as all prayers ascend to Me. Well, let Us hear what she has to say this time around.

Heavenly Father turned back to Debbie…

HF: OK Debbie, let me hear this favour of yours.

DEBBIE: Well HF, all I want is for You to issue a decree that would ban all housework. Just think about all the free time we would have to read our bibles, meditate and do good works. I know that this will surely bless Your holy heart.

Heavenly Father had that wise, all-knowing look in His eyes.

HF: Yes Debbie, I am almost persuaded except that I know where it all ends, just one word: Shopping!

DEBBIE: Shopping? Surely not, HF!

HF: Yes Debbie, shopping! With all that free time on your hands, you will shop for things you do not need and end up spending money you do not have. After maxing out your credit card you will then try to persuade your husband to give you the money to top it up again and, like we both know, this could end up in a quarrel.

Then you will come crying to Me and praying earnestly asking for money to pay your bills. You will even quote scriptures such as, *"My God shall supply all your needs according to His riches in glory by Christ Jesus"*[17], to back up your case. Then Lord Jesus will be forced to instruct you to return the items to the shops and Holy Spirit will have to busy Himself trying to maintain peace in your home. In the end, Holy Trinity will be embroiled in your little scheme and all because I abolished housework!

Bear in mind that the scenario I have just painted will be replicated in millions of homes around the world; with men, women and children doing it. So, your little prayer will end up as an almighty headache for Me.

In other words, Debbie, there is no chance that I will issue such a decree. So start putting your *gift of imagination* which I have heard so much about, to better use.

I was stunned at Heavenly Father's response. He even quoted scripture the right way up, something rarely done in Upside Down country. I found myself thinking of ways to appease the residents of Upside Down, especially those who had waited keenly with bated breath for a positive result. The solution to this difficult assignment came to me in a flash, thanks to Holy Spirit.

DEBBIE: My dear brothers and sisters, housework is one of those unfortunate things we have to do on this side of eternity. So, what we need to do is find ways of making it more interesting and fun. You could spend time singing praises to Almighty God (never mind the quality of your voice), dancing to music of your choice, and meditating. If you are a writer, poet or composer, you could keep a pen and paper handy ready to jot down any inspirational thoughts and ideas that come to mind. You would be amazed at just how easy it is to write an article, a sermon, lyrics, or even a book. Of course the housework may take a little longer, but I assure you it will be more rewarding. In fact, you just might start looking forward to doing it.

HF: Amazing! So, you do have this *gift of imagination* after all. You have the Holy Spirit to thank for bailing you out once again.

August 16
STITCHING

HF: Jesus, Holy Spirit, have you noticed that Debbie has been unusually quiet of late? I wonder what she is up to. Knowing her something must be brewing.

HOLY SPIRIT: She is, imaginatively speaking, busy stitching.

LORD JESUS: No way, not Our Debbie. She cannot stitch or sew anything to save her life!

HF: I better ask her what the final product will be. Let Us hope it will not be an ill-fitting *bubu*[18].

Heavenly Father decided that it was time to find out what His daughter was up to.

HF: Debbie, My dear daughter, what are you stitching and why? Do the shops no longer have clothes that you can buy, or have you run out of money?

DEBBIE: Oh HF, I can see that You do not have much confidence in my stitching abilities.

LORD JESUS: Let Us just say that when the gift of stitching was being given out, you were not exactly on the front row; more like at the back somewhere eating beans!

DEBBIE: I will yet surprise You with my stitching skills. But if You must know, as Holy Spirit said, I am imaginatively stitching. I reckon that if the Church is the bride of Christ which will be presented faultless without blemish or wrinkles at the Second Coming, then she has to wear a wedding gown befitting of the occasion.

Since the Church is very large, the wedding gown must be tailor-made so that it fits her perfectly. The way I see it, each generation of Christians must contribute their own stitches to ensure a perfect fit.

The gown has been designed by Holy Spirit, the Master designer Himself, and takes into consideration the need of every denomination and every type of Christian that has ever walked the face of the earth.

I have had a sneak preview of the dress and it is breathtakingly beautiful. The artistic work is out of this world; enough to make *Bezalel*[19] go green with envy. It is stitched with the finest of threads, and encrusted with sequins, pearls and precious stones.

HF: I like your analysis of this gown, but who is putting it together, and how exactly do you get to add your own stitches to it?

DEBBIE: Each Christian has been assigned a part of the gown to stitch. We are all under the supervision of Holy Spirit. The gown is stitched by our good deeds, acts of kindness, love, care and compassion. Each time we do a good deed, a stitch is sown. Every generation keeps adding to it until finally, the gown is ready for the Church to wear.

LORD JESUS: Now this is the *gift of imagination* at work. Well done Debbie. Keep on stitching and make sure you get all Upside Down citizens to join in.

HF: Yes, I am even becoming a believer in this gift. Holy Spirit should make sure that every Christian knows that they are supposed to be stitching, just like Debbie. I however want to carry out an inquiry as to why this *gift of imagination* is not in My holy textbook!

Both Lord Jesus and Holy Spirit looked at Heavenly Father in amazement. Even I was a bit confused.

Debbie: Eh, HF, wait a minute, has it occurred to You that you are actually the author of this gift. I mean, how did You create the universe out of nothing? To me, that was imagination at its very best! I am only following in Your footsteps; more a case of like Father, like daughter.

Heavenly Father had an excited, smile on face.

HF: My dear daughter, the truth has never sounded so true. I had this gift all along and here I was trying to carry out an enquiry on Myself!

I wondered what Heavenly Father would start getting up to now that I had reminded Him about His gift of imagination. Let us hope He does not create another universe!

~~~~~~

Every Christian has a role to play to help get the Church ready. Are you doing your bit? All you need to do is spread the good news of The Kingdom.

August 18
HEAVENLY PLANS

HOLY SPIRIT: HF, Jesus, I want to alert You to a rumour in one of My classes emanating from you know who: Debbie!

Heavenly Father and Lord Jesus did not look at all surprised.

HF: That cheeky girl needs to be checked! What has she said or done this time around?

HOLY SPIRIT: She has some grandiose plans for heaven and earth. But it might be better to ask her Yourself so that she can explain her position.

HF: My dear daughter, what is this I hear about you and your *great* plans?

DEBBIE: I have not done anything yet. I am just following the curriculum Holy Spirit designed for me. However, since You asked, I will tell You.

When I get to heaven, I will *butu*[20] for You, *butu* for Lord Jesus and butu for Holy Spirit. Then my troupe of dancers will usher me officially into Your presence. I will spend the first period of eternity camped at the foot of Your throne, enjoying the joy of being in Your presence at last and seeing the God who sees me.

LORD JESUS: There is nothing wrong with that Holy Spirit.

HOLY SPIRIT: That is only half of the story, let her finish.

Debbie, please continue.

DEBBIE: Well, after spending the first period getting to know Almighty God, I will proceed to spend the second period of eternity organising the Angels. This angelic re-organisation would have started here on earth as, before I depart the planet, I intend to organise the angels and saints. So in effect, I will only be doing in heaven what I have already started here on earth.

HF: This is getting interesting. What is wrong with the way the angels are currently organised?

DEBBIE: Nothing except that I have a vested interest in this re-organisation plan. I want the angels to help spread the message of my religion. Then I will spend the third period of eternity starting my very own religion.

HF: Debbie, will I see you again after the first period of eternity?

HOLY SPIRIT: HF at the rate at which she is going, You may have to book an appointment to see her.

LORD JESUS: I can see danger and this plan of hers is beginning to sound like another rebellion. As she is the main guru of her religion things may get a bit tricky. We have to find a way to scupper her plans.

HF: Indeed, but where does she get these ideas from? Who told her that there were periods in eternity anyway?

HOLY SPIRIT: She just dreams them up in that little mind of hers. Let Us shut her up from now to eternity. In fact, I have the perfect solution! I will keep her here on earth for as long as possible. I will grant her long life; a life longer than that of Methuselah's. Then, when she finally gets to heaven, she will be so tired that the only thing she will be looking forward to is eternal rest.

I could not believe my ears.

Debbie: Holy Spirit, that is not fair! Do you know how long I have been dreaming of getting to heaven? In fact, my whole being is already there. A long life is supposed to be a blessing but to live as long as Methuselah is pure punishment in my book.

Holy Spirit: Who said anything about it being fair?

HF, Jesus, when she finally gets to heaven, we should treat her to a feast of beans!

Heavenly Father and Lord Jesus thought Holy Spirit's plan was excellent. But what was this thing about a "feast of beans"?

Lord Jesus: Holy Spirit, what do you mean by a feast of beans?

Holy Spirit: Well, we all know how Debbie is really into her beans. So, I was thinking it would make a nice treat for her when she finally touches down in heaven. Yes, any beans would do: black-eyed beans, kidney beans, gungo peas, chick peas, broad beans, haricot beans, baked beans, green beans, red beans, yellow beans, brown beans, black beans, speckled beans, spotted beans; any type of beans from any part of the world will do. We just give her whatever mankind calls beans. And if we throw in all the Agatha Christie's Poirot films ever made, I can assure You that she will camp at the foot of Your throne forever, never to depart.

Heavenly Father and Lord Jesus thought this was a masterstroke of genius and gave a nod of approval.

HF: In fact, not only will we give her a feast of beans and Poirot movies; her heavenly mansion will also be made out of beans. I can assure You that, with all this in place, she will have no time for her religion or angelic re-organisation.

At this point the angels, who had been on tenterhooks concerning my plans, breathed a sigh of relief and resumed praise.

LORD JESUS: Out of curiosity, how do We cook the beans?

HOLY SPIRIT: We can curry it, boil it, bake it, roast it, stew it, puree it into *akara*[21] or *moin-moin*[22]; whichever way we cook it, I know the girl will eat it.

I could discern that my plans don yamutu yakari[23]. I had already started thinking about what I would be doing on earth for at least nine hundred and sixty nine years; a very depressing prospect from my perspective! As for a mansion of beans; I wailed, "how could Heavenly Father even consider doing that to me? I know I like beans but to miss out on all the other delicacies in heaven would be pure punishment!"

I had just about resigned myself to this fate when I heard Lord Jesus talking to Heavenly Father and Holy Spirit.

LORD JESUS: Truce; I need time out with My servant.

Heavenly Father and Holy Spirit granted the truce.

LORD JESUS: My dear Debbie, do you think you can actually bear to live on earth for over nine hundred years? As you very well know, Holy Spirit could decide to keep you on earth for as long as a thousand years if He pleases. Can you take that? Also, do you think you can handle an eternity of eating nothing else but beans, considering all the delicacies in heaven?

As for your religion and angelic re-organisation, I am sorry to disappoint you. It will never work in heaven, so concentrate your efforts on organising the saints and angels here on earth. I am sure that will take up a fair amount of your time, and then you can look forward to eternal rest in heaven.

DEBBIE: Thank you Lord Jesus, I will heed Your advice and concentrate my efforts here on earth.

HOLY SPIRIT: Debbie, hopefully you have now seen the light!

But just when I thought it was all over I heard the voice of Archangel Gabriel…

ARCHANGEL GABRIEL: Angelic re-organisation my foot! And a new religion in heaven! Whatever will I hear next? I do not know who she thinks she is. Grrr! God help us when millions of her kind invade heaven!

HF: Point of correction Archangel, I am actually expecting billions of her kind. So you better start preparing!

Archangel Gabriel burst into different tongues…

ARCHANGEL GABRIEL: *Oghene biko*[24]*! Oluwa sanu*[25]*! Chineke mme ebele*[26]*!* Lord have mercy!

DEBBIE: There goes HF speaking what is not into existence again.

Where will you spend eternity; with your Heavenly Father in light or separated from Him in darkness? The choice is yours but remember that you only have this life to make a decision!

August 20
MY APPEAL

DEBBIE: HF!

HF: Yes Debbie.

DEBBIE: I would like to appeal against the plans of Holy Spirit to keep me on earth for as long as a whopping nine hundred and sixty nine years; I mean that was how old Methuselah was before he died right? Please, I really do not want to live as long as that.

Heavenly Father glanced towards Lord Jesus and Holy Spirit.

HF: *Okpemu*[27], as they say in Urhobo land. Jesus, Holy Spirit, pay attention. It seems Debbie is about to protest against My plans.

Lord Jesus and Holy Spirit had seen this coming.

LORD JESUS: Maybe We should just ask her how long she wants to live.

HF: Good idea Jesus!

Heavenly Father turned His gaze towards Debbie…

HF: Debbie my dear daughter, so how long would you want to live on earth?

DEBBIE: I am glad You asked because I have it all worked out. First of all, I want to live the one hundred and twenty years guaranteed in the bible. After that I will be ready to come home to You. However, I intend to negotiate with You on a year by year basis on how many more years I want to live. This of course will depend on my usefulness on earth and, more importantly, how far I have gone with my angelic and saintly re-organisation plan.

HOLY SPIRIT: HF, if You want peace in heaven then You should stick to the original plan; nine hundred and sixty nine years and no less! Anyway, who told her she could negotiate how long she can live?

But I had not finished yet…

DEBBIE: Mankind has moved on and we now have many ways of circumventing Your will. So, if I am pushed, I will just do what some others have done; pay a visit to Switzerland or Holland. I am sure You have heard of euthanasia.

I could sense anger, never before witnessed in Upside Down country, in Heavenly Father's voice. He gave me a piercing look of reproach and spoke in a very stern voice...

HF: So you want to deliberately disobey My written commandment, *"You shall not murder"*[28], and engineer the taking of your own life, do you? What makes you think I will receive you in heaven? Be rest assured that both you and those who joined you in this evil will answer to Me!

A deep dread came upon me as I had not anticipated such a strong reaction from Heavenly Father. I know that whenever Heavenly Father starts to quote scripture the right way round in Upside Down country it is a sure sign that I have provoked Him to anger and was almost certainly about to see His red eye!

I was left quaking with fear, wondering what possessed me to even think of euthanasia in the first place. Unbeknown to me, I had touched a very raw nerve and began to wonder why the concept was slowly gaining acceptance in certain quarters.

"Well" I muttered to myself, "I am definitely not in the business of provoking Almighty God to anger. I know that the last time the children of Israel tried it they were sent into exile, and I have no intention of being sent to any undesirable place. What if Heavenly Father, knowing how much I hate the cold, decides to send me to the North or South Pole? Or worse still, what if He used me as a guinea pig to confirm the exact location of that strange place called Purgatory?"

I needed to say something before Heavenly Father took disciplinary action against me. So, meekly, in a tiny voice,...

DEBBIE: HF, please hold Your fire. I have had a change of heart. I will live as long as Holy Spirit decides I should.

But my repentance only lasted for a moment and I cheekily added...

DEBBIE: But HF, if I live as long as Methuselah or longer, when I finally do depart from planet earth I will not be coming back!

Holy Trinity wondered where Debbie was going with this.

HOLY TRINITY: Exactly what do you mean by that?

DEBBIE: According to the bible, Lord Jesus will come back again with His holy angels and the saints, to reign on earth. Well, I ain't coming back with them! I would have had my fill of planet earth and I opt to camp at the feet of HF. I will escort the triumphal party as far as the Pearly Gates of heaven and wave them bye-bye; that is as far as I will go.

HF: Even though it will be a new earth; something you have never seen before?

DEBBIE: Oh HF, can it compare with Your abode in heaven? I have waited too long to get to You. Besides, if all the angels and the saints go to earth who will keep You company? I would rather watch the proceedings on earth from the foot of Your throne!

Heavenly Father turned to Lord Jesus.

HF: Jesus, what shall I do with this daughter of mine? Can she not keep still for a minute?

LORD JESUS: Keep still? The girl is, spiritually speaking, hyperactive. She always comes up with ideas that seem to bewilder the human mind.

Lord Jesus turned to Holy Spirit.

LORD JESUS: HF, I suggest You hand her over to her Teacher to educate her on the new earth!

HOLY SPIRIT: Debbie My dear pupil, you have committed the ultimate sin in My sight and have disgraced Me your Teacher by your lack of knowledge. In fact, I am seriously considering demoting you. However, before I make My decision I would like you to explain, in your own words, what is written in the bible about the end time.

DEBBIE: Well, from the little I can recollect from Your lecture, a new earth and new heaven will be created as the old ones will pass away.

HOLY SPIRIT: Oh, so you actually went over your lecture notes? Now, if a new earth and a new heaven will be created, what makes you think HF will not opt to live on the new earth? Did He not say that He will be in the midst of His people, and He will be their light? I have a mind to leave you in the old heaven all on your own. I guess that would make a nice place for you to start your own religion!

Debbie: How can You separate me from HF after having waited so long to be with Him? Wherever He goes, I go; be it the new earth or the new heaven!

No one enjoys suffering. Euthanasia is however not the answer as it is a violation of God's commandment.

August 21
HEAVENLY KNITTING

DEBBIE: HF, how is the knitting coming along? Have You finished with my special requests yet?

Heavenly Father looked at Lord Jesus and Holy Spirit in amazement.

HF: Who told her I could knit?

Lord Jesus and Holy Spirit were just as surprised as Heavenly Father. After all, the bible did not seem to say anything about Him knitting!

HF: Aha, My dear daughter, where did you get the idea that I could knit from?

DEBBIE: Well, imaginatively speaking, I know You are excellent at knitting. Did you not knit Eve for Adam, Sarah for Abraham, Rebecca for Isaac, Ruth for Boaz and quite a few other couples together?

HF: Oh! You mean that type of knitting. Well, back in those days I used to knit for mankind. But as they have discovered romance, thanks to Mills and Boon and other such publications, I no longer get asked to knit. So understandably, I am a bit rusty as I get very few knitting requests. The few times that I do knit, it somehow gets thrown in My face when it ends in divorce over issues I would willingly heal. So you see, My dear daughter, I have left the knitting to mankind; let everyone carry on knitting for themselves.

DEBBIE: *Chei!*[29] HF, how could You stop knitting? Mankind desperately needs Your help. A few of us still have every confidence in Your knitting abilities and are totally satisfied with what You knitted for us. So, when can I expect the delivery of my special knitting requests?

HF: My dear daughter, I know of your special requests but alas, since the days when Solomon decided to *knit* seven hundred wives and three hundred concubines for himself, I learnt My lesson to only knit on request or in special circumstances.

DEBBIE: Look HF, Solomon was an extreme and special case. I mean the man practically snatched the knitting needles from Your hands.

HF: From where I am sitting, there are many male and female *Solomons*, who want to do the knitting themselves. So please, leave me out of this and let everyone continue doing their own knitting.

DEBBIE: HF, You cannot give up on us. We need help. Just look at the sorry state of the divorce statistics.

HF: So what do you intend to do about these divorce statistics?

DEBBIE: Wait a minute HF, what has this got to do with me? I just want You to knit a few people together. I did not envisage taking on such an enormous project for which I have no experience!

HF: *Oho!* So you want Me to knit but you are not prepared to do anything to keep the stitches in place. You know what? I will leave you to meditate on this for a while. Then you can come back to Me when you are ready to play your part.

I had really shot myself in the foot this time. What am I going to do? Why do I always seem to get myself involved in situations like this? Why couldn't I just keep my big mouth shut?

Suddenly, thanks to my Teacher, I had an idea. I recovered myself like the proverbial lizard that fell from the Iroko tree, and proceeded to address my fellow citizens of Upside Down...

DEBBIE: My dear brothers and sisters, as you have heard, HF is very reluctant to knit on our behalf, and who can blame Him. To help turn this situation around, I need us to do two things:

First of all, I need us to understand that the task of solving the divorce problem falls on each of us. Whether you knitted it yourself or not, it is your responsibility to try and make your marriage work. Seek help in times of trouble and deal with your marital difficulties.

Remember, divorce is not always the solution many seem to think it is. For those of you who are not yet married, love at first sight may sound romantic but that may not be the way to go as it could very easily go wrong.

Do not be a Solomon; pray and ask HF to do the knitting for you. Even though you may have to wait patiently, at least if He does the knitting you are guaranteed to be knit to the right person.

Secondly, I need all of us to imaginatively camp at the foot of HF's throne. Let us pray without ceasing until He resumes knitting for everyone. I am sure that by the time our fervent prayers ascend to Him, He will be left with no choice but to grant our petition.

So let us start now. Those of you in the northern hemisphere, imaginatively camp to the north of His throne and those in the southern hemisphere, take your position in the south.

LORD JESUS: HF can You take all this prayer fire? Would it not be easier for You to swiftly grant their petition? It is obvious that the girl is very serious about her saintly and angelic re-organisation for never in the history of mankind have the four corners of the earth united to speak with one voice. The last time they spoke with one voice was at the tower of Babel and that was to challenge You.

Heavenly Father looked at Lord Jesus, excitement in His eyes.

HF: Fire? What fire? I have waited since the creation of the earth for all My children to gather around and fellowship with Me. I am enjoying and basking in it, and I have a mind to make it last for as long as I want.

Heavenly Father then turned to Debbie...

HF: Debbie, your petition is granted!

There was a loud cheer from all the inhabitants of Upside Down. And once again the angels heaved a sigh of relief as they had already started wondering how they would handle the voluminous prayers from the four corners of the earth.

In the beginning God created them one flesh. "Therefore what God has joined together, let not man separate" (Matthew 19:6)

September 7
TRIALS WILL COME

DEBBIE: My dear fellow citizens of Upside Down, have you noticed a curious trend among some of our brothers and sisters? They seem to attribute anything happening in their lives, which they do not like, to Satan and his demons. This practice is so widespread that you often hear statements like, "Satan, you are a liar" or, "I reject that, in the name of Jesus". They are forever binding and casting out both real and imaginary demons. The way they carry on, you would think Satan is the one charting the course of their lives and not the Lord Jesus.

As HF Himself would say, it would appear that these people have never read their bibles, or maybe they're like Debbie who reads it upside down. According to the way these brethren think, every unpleasant thing in their lives must have taken Almighty God by surprise, and while He was not paying attention, the devil sneaked in through the back door.

To enlighten you further I'll use these three examples from the bible. First up is Joseph. According to this way of thinking, Almighty God blinked and momentarily lost concentration when Joseph was sold into slavery. This landed Joseph in Potiphar's house where his management experience began. Then to Joseph's consternation, Almighty God blinked yet again and he was accused of rape. Joseph was sent to prison where he continued to gain further management experience.

What about Naomi's situation in the book of Ruth? Almighty God must have completely lost control as He blinked so often that, before Naomi knew it, she had lost her husband and two sons in Moab and was left with two daughters-in-law, one of whom decided not to follow her back to Israel.

And In the case of Paul, it was simply one disaster after another as, after Almighty God called him to proclaim the gospel, He seemed to abandon him.

However, in all three scenarios we clearly see that in the end everything turned out for good. Joseph became the Prime Minister of Egypt; a position in which he saw the dreams that sold him into slavery come to pass. Almighty God used Naomi to orchestrate the marriage of her widowed daughter-in-law to a man named Boaz, and their great-grandson David, became the anointed King of Israel. And just as Almighty God had said, St Paul went on to accomplish his dream by spreading the gospel, and even took it to Rome, the nerve centre of the then super power: The Roman Empire. Do you get the picture?

This is where I have a problem with this way of thinking. The question is who decides what is good and what is bad? Do you really think HF is not in control of your situation? What makes you think that what you consider bad today will not turn out for your good tomorrow? Has God not promised in Romans 8:28 to work out everything for your good? When we attribute what He permits in our lives to shape us and bring us in line with His will to Satan, it is nothing but an affront to His person.

So my dear brothers and sisters loosen up and wake up; trials and tribulations are part of life. Though it is true that the devil and his demons are factors in some of our trials, must we flatter him further by actually acknowledging him? Be aware of his devices but keep your eyes firmly fixed on Lord Jesus.

Lord Jesus warned us, the apostles warned us, and in fact the entire bible is documented proof of some of the trials likely to befall us. As long as we dwell on planet earth, trials will come our way; it really does not matter what or who the origin is. One could say that it is part of our inheritance thanks to Adam and Eve. What really matters is how we deal with these trials.

Try to bear your trials with grace and fortitude; they will not last forever. HF has promised to set a limitation on them (1 Corinthians 10:13). If you do not want to go through trials then you may have to relocate to the planet Saturn or Jupiter, as it is possible that the beings that live there do not experience such.

Now, let us stop giving the glory due to Almighty God to the devil. As long as Lord Jesus is on the throne, we will overcome in the power of the Holy Spirit. That is a divine promise! So mind your language; think before you speak!

October 23
ANOTHER UPSIDE DOWN SPEECH

DEBBIE: My dear Upside Down residents, as you all know, I am always shooting my mouth off to Almighty God. Well, I have a confession to make; it has boomeranged on me! After deep meditation and further discernment, as well as taking stock of recent happenings in my life, it is with great humility that I have come to the conclusion that it is no use arguing with Holy Spirit about His guidance and counselling techniques. (*See my diary entry on July 17*). It just goes to show that it is a tough job to be wiser than your teacher, and if that teacher happens to be Holy Spirit then it is simply impossible. The truth is you can never be wiser than your heavenly Teacher.

I have come to realise that whether you are in for great or small blessings the *wahala*[30] is the same. So what is the point of going through trials and tribulations for small blessings when you can go through exactly the same for great blessings? Is it not better to just dive in; a case of "*in for a penny, in for a pound*" as they say in England?

Well, I have decided to register for Holy Spirit's course on Preparation for Great Blessing. So when the trials and tribulations come, and at some point they will come fast and thick, I will know why they are happening to me. At least hopefully I will not be taken by surprise like in times past.

For those Upside Down residents who are interested, Holy Spirit has whispered to me that He is enrolling students for this course as there are still a number of spaces in the class. So, if you are quick and want to enjoy great blessing, then now is your chance to register. However, do not say I did not warn you; prepare yourself for trials and tribulations, but be rest assured that you are not alone as Holy Spirit will guide you. There may be a few tears along the way but in the end, even after you have departed planet earth for heaven, the blessings will continue to flow. Some of us will enjoy some of the blessings during our life time but for many, the blessings will come after they have departed.

Whatever the case, we can trust Almighty God to keep His end of the bargain. Look at what He has done and what He continues to do for the descendants of Abraham. By the way, we are part of Abraham's blessing and that is what I call a mega blessing.

So, good luck on the course, if you decide to enrol, and see you in the library when we do our homework and course assignments. When the going gets tough, remember you are not alone in the class. Almighty God is right beside you, and all you have to do is listen to Holy Spirit, your Guide and Teacher.

Heavenly Father and Lord Jesus turn to Holy Spirit…

HF and LORD JESUS: Holy Spirit, what did you do to bring about such a change in Debbie?

HOLY SPIRIT: Aha. Now that would be telling. Let's just say, it is a trade secret of Mine!"

All the angels and saints in heaven praised Holy Spirit for His very excellent teaching, guiding and counselling techniques, and Archangel Michael could not resist the urge to add a little extra…

ARCHANGEL MICHAEL: I knew she would soon come unstuck; talking to Almighty God as if He were her mate. I cannot wait for her to get to heaven; then I will teach her a thing or two about reverence.

LORD JESUS: Sorry to disappoint you archangel, but by that time it will be too late. Anyway, you have a very long wait.

HOLY SPIRIT: A minimum of nine hundred and sixty nine years to be precise!

The Archangel Michael was too shocked for words.

November 1
WHY?

DEBBIE: HF, I have a few questions that I would like to ask You.

HF: Ah, Debbie My daughter, are you sure you do not want to ask your Teacher, Holy Spirit?

DEBBIE: The questions I have in mind concern You.

HF: Debbie, you may ask any question you like, but bear in mind that I may not answer any of them.

DEBBIE: Well, that will not stop me from asking.

My first question is about some of the hideous creatures on our planet. Why on earth did You create snakes? Apologies to all snake lovers out there and please pardon my ignorance, but what is their contribution to the well-being of mankind? Of what earthly value are they? Just take a look at all the trouble they have caused us. Was it not a snake that led to the fall of man? Although, knowing the wiles of the devil, any creature would have sufficed. But seriously speaking, I think extinction, rather than allowing it to crawl around on its belly, would have been the perfect punishment. I for one would not miss them one bit.

While on the subject of hideous creatures, did You really have to create the mosquito? Why oh why did Noah allow mosquitoes into the ark when all he needed to do was swat them? Maybe he was too busy keeping the peace between the lions and the sheep to bother with two tiny insects, but now the mosquito is one insect the world could do without. Just look at all the misery this tiny insect has caused.

Thanks to the mosquito, nearly one million people world-wide die from malaria each year. Most of these are children under the age of five, and so many more people are at risk. It just seems like the only reason this insect exists is to spread nothing but disease.

Billions have been spent on medication, lotions, potions, repellents, sprays, gels, coils and nets, yet to little avail. We are forever taking Sunday to Sunday medicines and other prophylaxis. It has, and continues to out manoeuvre man, scientists and all, by quickly thwarting all efforts to defeat it. Each time we celebrate a new wonder drug, the mosquito ups the ante and quickly adapts. This tiny insect has simply proved too difficult to pin down.

This is the one time we need You to intervene; exercise Your power and do a *product recall* as the Maker. You will be doing mankind, especially those living in the tropics, a massive favour if You could possibly make this insect extinct as swiftly as possible. If You like I could make a convincing case for this move as it is a multi-billion pound industry. The lotions, the potions and other products that have been made to fight the mosquito are endless. I tip my hat to the scientists waging war against this pest on our behalf. However, the time has come for a change in tactics.

Mankind seems to have tried everything, but what about prayer? HF, could You please give us insight into what we need to do to win this war against the mosquito and malaria?

To those scientists out there who are still trying to revive the dinosaur; let the mosquito be a lesson to you all. For very good reasons, still unknown to man, dinosaurs are extinct. They obviously never made it into Noah's ark as; judging from their remains the ark itself was hardly big enough for one dinosaur let alone the two required. Right now man and beasts are living in harmony; at least no beast has been known to overpower man just yet, except the mosquito.

Man's war against the mosquito is still raging as I write. We are currently engaged in a game of chess with the mosquito and hopefully, eventually we will win and overpower it. If the film Jurassic Park is anything to go by, then I would strongly advise that we leave dinosaurs well alone unless we want man to be extinct.

I turned to address the residents of Upside Down country.

DEBBIE: There are other downright ugly creatures living on our planet and I sometimes wonder what HF was thinking when He created them. I will not bore you with their names as I am sure you have the ones you like and hate, and it is quite possible that what I consider ugly from a human perspective are an epitome of beauty in the animal kingdom.

In fairness to HF these animals and creatures are well adapted to their environments. But like you may have probably guessed by now, if HF had given me the same task as Noah, many of these creatures would never have made it on to the ark going by my selection criteria.

My fellow Upside Down residents, I do love some animals; the zebras, lions, pandas, antelopes, reindeers, majestic birds, the beautiful and elegant whales, seals, dolphins and other fish of the sea are some of my favourites. It is just that I feel like griping to HF about some of the mean and nasty creatures in our world, especially those creepy crawlies; insects and creatures that bite and sting for no reason whatsoever. Ugh! I get goose bumps just thinking about them.

Turning back to Heavenly Father

DEBBIE: Well, that's me done. Any comments HF?

Heavenly Father had been conspicuously silent during Debbie's rant, and after some more silence He decided to respond.

HF: Debbie My dear daughter, I have heard all you have said, and here is My take on the matter. If I made the snake, the mosquito and all the other creatures that you dislike extinct, not only would it affect the ecological balance, but more importantly, someone somewhere would one day make the same argument for another creature. At this rate, I might as well make Myself extinct!

My creation is an expression of who I am. My work of creation is complete; take it or leave it! I know there are many people out there who would love Me to be extinct. Well, tough! As you would say, "I ain't going nowhere!"

ARCHANGEL GABRIEL: The girl just never learns. First she took on Holy Spirit and lost, and now she has turned her attention to HF. Oops, Lord have mercy! What have I just said? She has even got me saying HF. I tell you, the girl is infectious. God help us when the whole world starts saying the same.

In the beginning God did not give mankind the solution to every problem. He has however made the necessary knowledge and wisdom available to help mankind work things out through various avenues, such as scientific research, so that he can fulfil His purpose and have dominion over all the creatures of earth. (Genesis 1:28)

November 29
CELIBACY MIX-UP?

Debbie: Holy Spirit, how do You explain the celibacy and serving the Lord mix-up?

Holy Spirit: *Ewo[31]!* Jesus, HF, I need help. If I choose to answer this question the egos of many will be severely bruised. Besides, I am provoked; this is certainly a sore point with Me.

HF: Debbie, have you ever read your bible from cover to cover?

Debbie: Yes, a few times.

HF: Good. That means you should know what is written in it. So My very clever daughter, when was the priesthood instituted and who was the very first high priest?

"Who sent me on this errand?" I muttered to myself. I tried to answer Heavenly Father's question...

Debbie: Well, in the book of Genesis there is a reference to Melchizedek as a priest of the Most High God. However, I believe the priesthood was officially instituted when You made Aaron the first High Priest. You also ordained Aaron's sons as priests to serve under him to continue the priestly tradition.

HF: Very good! Now, what did I promise Aaron and his sons in the book of Exodus chapter 40 verses 14-15?

Now I was beginning to get a bit flustered.

DEBBIE: You promised them *"an everlasting priesthood throughout their generation"*.

LORD JESUS: The girl is indeed very sharp.

HF: Excellent Debbie. Now, tell Me, how were Aaron and his sons meant to be priests forever if they were celibate? How do celibate priests have descendants that would serve Me forever?

Heavenly Father knew I was struggling but He continued anyway…

HF: And while you think about that, I am sure you know that I also set the Levites apart to minister to Me forever, but do you remember Me commanding any of them, man or woman, to be celibate?

DEBBIE: No.

HF: Did I actually command any man or woman to give up their right to marriage in order to serve Me?

DEBBIE: I choose to pass on this question. However, I do not remember reading any commandment to this effect in Your holy textbook. So, where did this celibacy and serving You mix-up stem from?

HF: You tell Me, because personally I am baffled.

DEBBIE: Could it be the interpretation of Lord Jesus' words in Matthew 19:12?

LORD JESUS: Were My words tantamount to a blanket policy of celibacy for nuns, monks and priests?

DEBBIE: Now that you say it, no!

Or could it be traced back to what St Paul said in the book of 1 Corinthians chapter 7?

HF: But was Paul giving a command or was he simply expressing a personal opinion? And if it was a command, should it override My own?

DEBBIE: It is true, St Paul was expressing an opinion, and he did make it clear that this was not a commandment.

HF: Now my daughter, help me out here. Where, oh where in the entire bible, or in all creation for that matter, did I actually command any woman or man to be a nun, a monk or a celibate priest in order to serve me?

DEBBIE: I don't know as I do not recall coming across it anywhere in Your holy textbook. How what St Paul wrote came to be interpreted as a blanket policy and commandment of Almighty God in certain quarters of Christendom is a mystery to me. It could be that Your commandment was lost in translation.

HF: Is this not a case of *"teaching as doctrines the commandments of men"*[32]?

DEBBIE: Ah Lord God, I agree with you as it would appear that there has been a *"laying aside of Your commandments to uphold the tradition of men".*[33]

HF: There they go, men and women burning with, and suppressing passion which should be consummated in marriage; some committing adultery, others committing fornication and other sins too shameful to be mentioned. How many more cases of sexual abuse must I endure in all the continents of the world for something I never commanded in the first place?

How much more of My money will be spent on paying compensation to abused victims? Who will bear the enormous cost of the blighted and damaged lives? Those who are now incapable of giving or receiving love; those that struggle to become good husbands and fathers; those that have now rejected Me because of the evil done in My name? What about the women who were ill advised into taking vows of celibacy which I did not command?

It was time for me to address the residents of Upside Down country again.

DEBBIE: Can you feel the deep hurt and anger of HF? The time has come to review compulsory celibacy for priests, monks and nuns within Christendom. We have gone too far; upholding what He did not command in the first place and making it into an unbreakable law. The fact that this has gone on for hundreds of years does not make it right.

As most of Christendom can testify, it is very possible to be married and still serve God. The two are not mutually exclusive. Most world renowned evangelists, preachers and bible teachers are married. HF would not institute marriage then deny some of His children the joy it brings so that they can serve Him.

If we do not begin to undo this man-made law, we will force God's hand; He will surely act to protect His name and uphold His just, righteous and true commandments. He may be longsuffering but that does not mean that we should take His patience for granted. When it comes to God's decrees and commandments, we should only do what He says in His holy textbook.

Remember, it may take God hundreds of years to act, but act He will. So, follow the advice in the book of Proverbs

30:5-6: *"Every word of God is pure;... ...do not add to His word, lest He rebuke you, and you are found a liar."*

December 12
HELP IN TIME OF NEED

HF: Debbie My dear daughter, how are you getting on with the diet plan? Have you lost any weight of late?

Holy Spirit looked at Lord Jesus in amazement.

HOLY SPIRIT: Jesus, did You just hear that? It seems HF wants to get involved in Debbie's diet plan; something I have made up My mind not to have anything to do with.

LORD JESUS: HF, don't You have enough trouble without adding Debbie's diet plan to Your workload? Take My advice, leave Debbie and her diet well alone. If Holy Spirit, her teacher is not getting involved, it just might be better to steer clear. Why would You want to damage Your holy reputation?

As You very well know, Debbie practices the *See Food Diet*; she sees food and she eats it! No matter how much she eats, when the mood takes her she always has room for more. I, her Saviour, totally agree with Holy Spirit; I am not getting involved!

HF: I have heard You Jesus. But as her Father, I have to support her.

DEBBIE: Thank You HF for Your support. I discerned long ago that Holy Spirit and Lord Jesus were not getting involved in my diet plan. I will try my very best not to damage Your holy reputation on this one. But, as You already know, Christmas, the season of good cheer, is just around the corner so I will need Your help sooner rather than later.

HF: Aha, Jesus, Holy Spirit, I am beginning to understand why both of You decided not to get involved. Christmas is definitely not the best time for any diet plan, and knowing Debbie she will go overboard and then heap all the blame on Me.

Lord Jesus: HF, I am glad that You have seen the light. The truth is Debbie is so bad at sticking to a diet plan, especially during the Christmas season. In fact Holy Spirit had to come up with a code to help her.

On one occasion, she not only ate enough for Britain and Nigeria, she proceeded to eat for North and South America until Holy Spirit, realising that all His efforts had been undone, screamed in frustration, "STOP!" He has since tried to help her resist this temptation but to little avail. He now calls her North and South.

HF: Debbie My daughter, I love you very much but on this occasion you are on your own.

Debbie: Has it occurred to Holy Trinity that I could actually sue You for child abandonment? For the records, I will not be the first person to do this as I hear a man in the U.S. state of Nebraska did so not too long ago. Unfortunately for him though, the judge threw the case out as he did not think himself competent to hear it. They were also unable to serve You Notice as they did not know Your address. I however will not be making the same mistakes, and I have evidence to back my case.

HF: And what evidence might that be?

DEBBIE: Did You not say that *"I will never leave you nor will I forsake you"*? And for the records, this statement is repeated at least five times in Your holy textbook. The Lord Jesus made my case even easier as He also said *"I am with you always, even to the end of the age"*[34].

HOLY SPIRIT: The girl has done her homework. What shall We do?

HF: We need a lawyer to defend Us.

Holy Spirit looked at Lord Jesus.

HOLY SPIRIT: A lawyer? You have an Advocate sitting right next to You in the person of Jesus. I am sure He can defend Us.

LORD JESUS: Ah, um, there is a bit of a snag with My defence. We did say what she quoted so there is no getting away from that, and We cannot go back on Our word. In short, the girl is right. We have no case, so let Us take the smart option and support her.

HF: Jesus, is there no get-out clause for Us? Please search the scriptures again.

LORD JESUS: Look, the only get-out clause We have is if she is disobedient and even then it is a weak one because, should she repent, We are once again bound by Our word to forgive and do as she asks. I need not tell you that Debbie can quote the scriptures the right way round too when it comes to backing up her argument. So let Us kill this case.

DEBBIE: My fellow Upside Down residents, I have shown you the way. You may, if you wish, sue Holy Trinity but make sure you have a watertight case as He has a formidable Advocate who will take you apart if you do not.

The only way you can win is if you base your case on any of God's promises written in the good book as you can be sure that He will ALWAYS honour His word. He has never failed anyone yet and He never will.

However, remember that Almighty God does have one get-out clause: DISOBEDIENCE! If you have disobeyed Him do not bother trying to sue Him as He will no longer be duty bound to keep His word, unless you repent.

Are you finding it hard to stick to your diet or exercise plan? Are you having a tough time kicking a habit? Pray and ask the Lord to help you.

December 15
DELIVERANCE AND THE BLOOD

DEBBIE: I feel I must gripe, and say all that is in my heart about some of the curious and strange things that some of our brothers and sisters do.

One thing that bothers me is the craze to break curses. These brothers and sisters of ours are forever breaking the curse of poverty, the curse of unemployment, the curse of lack of promotion at work, the curse of financial indiscipline and greed and the curse of laziness. They no longer wait on Holy Spirit for insight and revelation. They assume that since that brother's problem was as a result of a curse, then all the problems they face must be the same.

Some of our brothers and sisters are forever seeking deliverance from every known human problem. Deliverance here, deliverance there, deliverance everywhere! The rate at which they are going they will soon be asking for deliverance from the Holy Spirit, and it would not surprise me if one day someone asked for the curse of not spending quality time with God to be broken. Hello! There is no shortcut to spiritual growth, and I personally do not believe that breaking curses is the answer.

Another strange thing currently in operation in Christendom is the fashionable prayer to cover anything and everything with the blood of Jesus.

Some of our brothers and sisters are experts at this. They

cover themselves, their homes, and their food with the blood of Jesus. When they are travelling, they cover the cars, the buses, the trains and planes; when they are ill they cover the hospital. The list is endless! As they say in Urhobo land *emuakpor Oghene mhe!*[35]

They have almost bled the Lord Jesus dry. Sometimes I wonder if He can still spare a drop to wash away my sins; after all that is all I need. The last time I checked, Lord Jesus shed His blood to take away our sins. Can someone out there please tell me where it is written in the bible that we need to cover everything with the blood of Jesus? Or have I missed something?

Did the Apostles Peter and John tell the lame beggar at the Beautiful Gate of the temple that, *"Silver and gold we do not have, but we cover you in the blood of Jesus, be healed"*?[36] Of course not; they pronounced healing in the name of Jesus. So, can you begin to see how absurd this prayer is? Let us get back to true biblical prayers that honour Almighty God and allow Holy Spirit to teach us to pray. Covering everything with the blood of Jesus may make us feel good but, as far as I am concerned, it is akin to treating the sacred and precious blood of the Lamb as a magic potion.

His blood cleansed us from all sin and unrighteousness; it is the basis of the new covenant that gives us access to HF. It is not to be treated like the blood of sacrificed bulls and goats. The power is in the name of Jesus! His name is sufficient to meet all our needs for all eternity. It is *"at the name of Jesus every knee should bow, of those in heaven, and of those on earth, and of those under the earth"*[37]. God will not give us something that will not accomplish His purpose.

HF has staked His reputation on the power of the name

of Jesus so let us use it. The name of Jesus has served the Church well down the ages and I have no doubt that it will continue to do so.

HF: Amazing! I could not have said it any better Myself. Who put Debbie up to it?

LORD JESUS: Not Me, I was troubleshooting somewhere in Africa.

HOLY SPIRIT: Certainly not I as I momentarily blinked and somehow missed it. That leaves only You HF.

HF: Why do I get this uncanny feeling that the girl can read My mind?

HOLY SPIRIT: She spends too much time with You and to quote her, *"God is as clear as daylight until He wants to stitch you up. When He stitches you up, you will be the last to know"*. In other words, it is not that difficult to read Your mind sometimes.

LORD JESUS: There you go HF, she knows a thing or two about You.

Well done Debbie, let us see if the rest of Christendom will allow Holy Spirit to teach them how to pray.

Archangel Gabriel and the other angels muttered to themselves, "Almighty God needs to anoint more like her".

December 22
PRAY THE RIGHT WAY

DEBBIE: Saint Abraham, Saint Isaac, Saint Jacob, pray for me. Saint Moses, Saint Joseph, Saint Peter, Saint Paul, pray for me. Saint James, Saint Mary, Saint Agnes, Saint Agatha, pray for me. Saint Christopher, Saint Joan, Saint Francis, Saint Theresa pray for me. Archangel Gabriel, Archangel Michael, all the angels of God, pray...

LORD JESUS: Debbie, what exactly are you doing?

DEBBIE: Lord Jesus, I am busy praying.

LORD JESUS: Did you say, "Praying"? Who taught you to pray in this way? How many saints and angels do you intend to summon to pray for you? Anyway, what is your petition and why can't you tell HF yourself?

DEBBIE: Well, to be honest I cannot recall anyone teaching me to pray like this. I just picked it up from some of my brothers and sisters. It is actually a church tradition that has been passed down for many generations, and believe me Lord Jesus, it is a recognised practice in Christendom.

Anyway, the more saints and angels I can summon, the more people I will have praying for me. The way I see it this can only mean quick, if not instant answers to my prayers.

Now that you ask, I seem to have lost track of my original petition but I am sure the saints still remember. See, that is another advantage of getting the saints and angels involved.

Heavenly Father looked shell-shocked.

HF: Wonders will never cease.

Debbie My dear daughter, how does calling on the saints and angels work? Do they have the power to answer your prayers?

DEBBIE: See HF, I think this is a question You should ask certain cardinals and bishops because I cannot claim to be an authority on this matter. However, from the little I know, when I ask the saints to pray for me, they take my petitions to Lord Jesus who in turn takes it to You and the chain is complete. The truth is I cannot claim to completely understand it. I am desperate, and from where I stand, if it works for some then there must be some merit in it.

HF: Holy Spirit is this what have You been teaching Debbie on prayer?

HOLY SPIRIT: Well HF, once again she embarrasses Me. I am currently considering two options; either to strike her with dumbness so as to put a check on these prayers of hers, or to actually kill her with My own bare hands so that she can personally explain her reason for daring to bring My holy name and teaching into disrepute.

The very thought that My name could be dragged into this way of praying beggars belief. These children of Yours pray to the saints and the angels, and somehow believe that, as long as they remember to add the name of Jesus at the end of the prayer, it is ok.

LORD JESUS: First let Us get to the bottom of this matter.

So Debbie, can you explain why you ask dead saints, some of whom have been dead for hundreds of years, to pray for you, instead of allowing them to rest in peace?

DEBBIE: Well, technically speaking they are not dead as they are with You in heaven and therefore have a strong influence on what happens around Your throne; at least that is the impression I get. In fact these saints are so powerful that many a miracle has been ascribed to them. It has also been alleged that some of them have appeared to those who prayed to them!

Holy Spirit shook His head in disappointment.

HOLY SPIRIT: HF, Lord Jesus, can you see the foolishness in her thinking?

Debbie My dear pupil, you have never been to heaven, and apart from what has been revealed to you through scripture and your vivid imagination, you do not even know how things work up here. However, since you are so clever, can you tell Me where it is written in the bible that the living saints should ask the dead saints to pray for them? And while you are at it, can you name one person in the bible who actually prayed to an angel?

DEBBIE: We all know that the bible is a big book that has many versions. But to answer Your question, I have not come across any of these situations in any of the versions that I own. However, what I can recollect is that prayer should be offered for all the saints, that is the body of believers.

I was being forced to reconsider how I pray, especially as I was once again in danger of being expelled from Holy Spirit's school. I quickly turned to

DEBBIE: Dear brothers and sisters, I do not know who taught us to pray to, or call on, dead saints and angels but it seems like the time has come for us to review this practice and bring it to an end. It is no use asking dead saints to pray for us when we are surrounded by living saints who would most certainly do a better job. Besides, these saints, as famous as they may have been, were mere servants of Christ.

Come to think of it, why ask these dead saints to pray for us when we have direct access through the Lord Jesus? What is the point of having *"a High Priest, who is seated at the right hand of the throne of the Majesty in the heavens"*[38] if all we plan to do is call on dead saints? If Lord Jesus and Holy Spirit are continually making intercession for us[39], why do we need to ask dead saints to pray for us?

My dear brothers and sisters, now we know the truth, we should always pray to Lord Jesus. If your need is so great and extra help is required, do not hesitate to ask the living saints in your church, fellowship or home group to join you in prayer. That is one of the reasons why they are there.

Leave the dead saints alone! Let them rest in peace for they are in the bosom of father Abraham. The lives they lived are examples that we can learn from; a legacy that we should always cherish. Let us read about them and emulate them, but whatever you do, do not pray to them or ask them to pray for you.

Now that you have been told do not be surprised if when next you ask Saint Christopher, Saint Francis or Saint Theresa to pray for you, you get an unnerving silence from heaven!

As for praying to the angels; I do not know how this started as they have no power to grant your petitions. They are messengers of God and, like us, fellow servants of the Almighty. So please do not pray to them.

Once again the saints and angels in heaven heaved a sigh of relief and thanked God for Debbie. Then they asked Holy Spirit to anoint more like her to spread the good news.

Archangel Michael: Thank God that someone finally has the courage to speak up on some of these strange practices in Christendom.

Heavenly Father, could each angel be given a copy of this book when it is published. We like some of the things she writes about and it will definitely come in handy in educating some of Your saints.

HF: That should not be a problem. In fact, I will need to get a copy Myself once it has been published.

LORD JESUS: You are a tad too late HF. I have already put My name down for a copy.

HOLY SPIRIT: Now, now, one copy should do for Us.

DEBBIE: Fellow Upside Down residents, it would appear that between Holy Trinity and His angels, this diary of mine has already sold out before hitting the press. I really hope there will be some copies left for us.

When I set out to write "My Diary of Upside Down Prayers", it was with the intention of writing a gospel according to *moi*, Saint Deborah, but it seems that I have inadvertently written a book according to Almighty God.

This book was meant to be the new bible for the converts of my religion, but it seems like Almighty God is my first convert. I guess a girl cannot aim any higher than that right? If this book has put a smile on the face of My Heavenly Father then I can only thank my Teacher, Holy Spirit.

All I can say is, "To all you followers of mine out there; make sure you beat the angels to your nearest Christian bookshop so that you do not miss out on a copy". Better still; simply place your order online.

THE QUESTION & ANSWER SESSION

Venue: Goshen Theatre, Holy Spirit's Bible College

Holy Spirit: Debbie!

My alarm bells started ringing. Why was Holy Spirit calling me?

Debbie: Yes Lord, did You call?

Holy Spirit: Yes I did. I want to leave you in charge of My class for a jiffy.

Now I was panic stricken.

Debbie: Holy Spirit are You sure about this? I mean, I know I take the mickey sometimes about Your teaching, guidance and counselling techniques, but to actually take charge of Your class? That is way over my head. I would prefer to leave it to the experts, like You!

Holy Spirit: See Debbie, you will be doing Me a big favour because, thanks to you, all sorts of questions are ascending to the throne of Almighty God; questions concerning your new country, Upside Down, and its language.

Since you are its originator, I thought it would be a good idea if you could answer these lingering questions yourself.

By the way, I have taken the liberty to gather the residents of Upside Down, heaven and earth to hear this session.

Debbie: So where will You be while I take this class?

Holy Spirit: Not to worry Debbie, I will be somewhere at the back of the class watching and listening to your every word.

Debbie: What about HF and Lord Jesus?

Holy Spirit: Remember, *"where two or three are gathered together in My name, I am there in the midst of them"*[40]. So, they will also be in the class.

Debbie: Ok, if You put it like that. But what if the questions become complex and too theological? As You know, I am not a theologian.

Holy Spirit: I will deal with any theological questions you have difficulty answering, but I seriously doubt that will happen.

I paused and took a deep breath.

Debbie: Ok Lord, I will take the class.

So, I turned to brief all those in the class…

Debbie: My fellow residents of Upside Down, as you have heard, I am not a theologian so should you have any theological questions, kindly direct them to your vicar, priest, pastor, bishop or cardinal. Failing that, direct them to the Holy Teacher oops, I mean Holy Spirit. Remember, this is not a normal class; it is a question and answer time and I am standing in for this session only. So, let us begin.

BROTHER JACK: How do you relate to each person of the Godhead?

DEBBIE: Almighty God is Trinity. He reveals Himself as God the Father, God the Son and God the Holy Spirit, so I relate to Him in that way.

Heavenly Father or HF, as I like to call Him, is a perfect father and there is no other father like Him. I have known Him all my life. He is loving, dependable and always on hand to give out treasures of wisdom from His very vast experience of dealing with mankind. I love HF and I can always trust Him. He always has time for me; He is never in a hurry nor does He hush me up. At every period of my life, the critical ones, the difficult ones, He has always been there. When I overstepped the mark and transgressed His commandments, He chastised me and He drew me back to Himself with His loving arms.

Being a material girl, I love HF on the materialistic front because He pays my bills as long as they are within reason and part of His will for my life. He meets my needs generously and He never grumbles. I tell you, if you are rightly related to Almighty God, you can submit any wish list, heart's desire list, want list and those needs you just cannot verbalise, to Him and He will make it a reality with no quibbles. At least that is my experience. He sure knows how to pamper and spoil a girl. I can only say, try Him out for yourself and let me know how you get on.

One more thing; if all fathers were like HF, there definitely would be no teenage crisis. He knows how to lovingly, yet firmly, deal with stubborn and difficult children, and I should know because I was one of them. Remember, He has thousands of years of experience.

Sister Lizzie: I kind of understand HF but what about Lord Jesus?

Debbie: Everyone needs a best friend; someone you can tell those inner secrets and fears; someone who has been through exactly what you are facing. Lord Jesus is the best friend anyone could ever wish for. Whenever you are unsure of whom to talk to, take it to Jesus. He is always there with a listening ear. The good thing is that He is comprehensively experienced in both heavenly and earthly matters. So, whatever the situation, crisis or confusion, be rest assured that your Best Friend is always there to lend a helping hand.

But apart from being my best friend, He is first and foremost my Lord and Saviour. He directs the course of my life. Wherever He sends me I go, and whatever He tells me to do, I really try and do.

Brother Ted: OK, so what about Holy Spirit?

I was tempted to say; "If after reading everything I have written you do not know who Holy Spirit is and what He does, then I would suggest that you start reading again". But after a brief pause I decided to be a good teacher and answer the question.

Debbie: Holy Spirit is the Holy Teacher. He teaches me everything I need to know about HF, about Lord Jesus and also about Himself. He also teaches me all I need to know about life. Like Lord Jesus, He is comprehensively experienced on all issues, and even though it seems His first earthly manifestation was on the day of Pentecost, He has been around for quite some time; before time began to be precise. Holy Spirit will be with us forever so you better get used to having a personal relationship with Him.

Holy Spirit helps me understand scripture, as well as other complexities in life that confound me. He freely gives me His gifts, including the gift of imagination. *(This is currently not recorded in the bible which is a gross omission. But I think HF is looking into that)*. Holy Spirit teaches everyone. It does not matter if you are a child or an aged grandfather or grandmother, there is always something to learn at His school.

The best thing about Holy Spirit, at least to me, is that His patience knows no bounds. He is very gentle in His teaching methods and allows you to learn at your own pace. He even waits until you have understood what He wants you to learn.

However, I must warn you that Holy Spirit is very economical with His teaching time. What He teaches you, He expects you to teach your children and grandchildren, if and when you have any. He also expects you to teach anyone He sends your way.

From my experience I have come to realise that Holy Spirit actually prefers one to one teaching as this helps build a personal relationship.

And how could I forget! Holy Spirit also teaches me how to pray, and what to pray for. He is my Counsellor and my Comforter; He gives me the kind of counsel and wisdom that money simply cannot buy.

SISTER SARAH: Going by your approach, it seems like you have separated God.

DEBBIE: Well, perhaps, but God is One! If you have accepted Lord Jesus into your heart, you have all three persons of Holy Trinity. Try as I might, I cannot separate

Him.

Most Christians do not have a problem with having a relationship with a Triune God. However non-Christians do and this is understandable as they do not know Him and therefore do not have a relationship with Him.

Brother Philip: Who taught you how to speak the Upside Down language?

Debbie: I would say, "I taught myself." It all started with my love of comedy. Whenever I saw or read something funny and there was no one around to share it with, I would share it with Holy Spirit. Holy Spirit would then get HF and Lord Jesus involved and the language just kind of grew from there. I enjoyed it so much that it gradually became a part of me. It also made me more aware of Holy Trinity as I realised that I could talk to Him wherever and whenever I wanted to. I learnt to share not only jokes, but issues that I thought needed His attention.

Sister Becky: Were you not afraid of being accused and stoned for blasphemy, or even struck down by lightning?

Debbie: At one time it did cross my mind that, because of my cheeky attitude towards Almighty God, fire could stream down from Mount Sinai and consume me. As for being stoned for blasphemy, I had to apologise to Moses and told him that Lord Jesus had made all the difference and gave an overriding instruction that we can relate to HF as Abba, father, with childlike simplicity, faith and obedience.

I know that if I told my earthly father half of what I told my Heavenly Father, I would get licked. But, like I said before, there is no other father like HF. In fact, He is the only father I know who disciplines perfectly; how He does it beats even my imagination.

As you can see for yourself, I am still very much alive and have not yet been consumed by fire or lightning, neither have I been stoned for blasphemy. I guess it has something to do with Lord Jesus and Holy Spirit who are constantly interceding on my behalf.

SISTER AGNES: Do you ever pray normally?

DEBBIE: Of course I do, and most of my Upside Down prayers flow from my personal time of devotion. I read my bible, meditate and pray like Christians should do, but I usually end up speaking Upside Down language.

Sometimes I believe HF prefers me speaking Upside Down because He knows I am able to express myself better in this way. I must however say a big thank You to Almighty God for allowing me to relate to Him in this way. It has made a tremendous difference in my life and in my understanding of Him.

BROTHER SOLOMON: So why did you decide to write down your Upside Down prayers?

DEBBIE: Each time I spoke Upside Down language it made me smile or laugh out loud. Those around me could not understand why. They must have thought I was going nuts. Anyway, because of this I thought I had better write some of it down for my children, to at least explain my strange behaviour. I did not know that I had so much to write. The material just grew with each passing day such that my little note book could no longer handle it. I decided to type it up on my computer and share it with some friends. They read it and persuaded me to publish it.

BROTHER ANTHONY: What would you say are the benefits of speaking Upside Down language?

DEBBIE: I would say, mental and physical relaxation; being free to be yourself and express your innermost thoughts to HF without the need to be formal; being filled with the joy and peace of Almighty God.

Even in the midst of trials, Holy Spirit suddenly brings an assurance to mind that not only makes you relax, but also helps you see the funny side. Before you know it you will find yourself smiling and laughing through your struggles. Sometimes that is all it takes and within a short while you have found a way out of your trial.

I would advise all you readers out there to start speaking Upside Down because in my opinion, it is indeed the language of heaven. It has enabled me to enjoy God; something I had never experienced until I started speaking this language.

The way I see it, if we are going to spend eternity with Almighty God, we might as well start learning how to enjoy Him now.

SISTER ALICE: I like the way you assign different statements to each Person. How do you decide who says what?

DEBBIE: That is quite simple really. It is based on the character of each Person, and what I see them doing both in my life and in the world around me. As a rule of the thumb, if the words the Lord ministered to my heart are fatherly, stern or disciplinary, I assign them to HF. If they are more like words spoken between friends, or what a master would say to a servant, I would assign them to Lord Jesus. If they sound like what a teacher would say to a pupil, I simply assign them to Holy Spirit. In short I relate to HF as a daughter, to Lord Jesus as a friend and servant, and to Holy Spirit as a pupil.

Brother Danny: You must have read a lot to acquire all this knowledge. What would you recommend I do to get started?

Debbie: The answer to this question is two-fold.

First of all I would advise that you try and read your bible, the holy textbook, from cover to cover a few times. You need to meditate on the contents of the holy textbook. Meditate, meditate some more and then meditate even more; Me-di-ta-te until it hurts!

Take time to read bible commentaries and other good Christian literature; they will help you understand the Persons of the Trinity more. And then, to finish it off, spend oodles and oodles and oodles and oodles of time in the presence of God in prayer.

Heavenly Father could no longer hold back.

HF: Holy Spirit, are You sure You do not want to take control of Your class? Debbie is trying to give Me a bad name!

Holy Spirit: Now Debbie, exactly how many bible commentaries have you read?

Debbie: Ah, um, well, none actually. But I did say the answer to this question was two-fold, and what I have just said is the right way up. The second part is the Upside Down answer, and since this is the Upside Down country, we rarely do things the right way up.

I turned to Brother Danny.

DEBBIE: So my dear Brother Danny, in answer to your question you should just come as you are. Start sharing your life with Almighty God. Read your bible and other Christian literature to help you know God better but you need not overdo it. I mean how many bible commentaries must you read before you start talking to Almighty God? I am sure you have heard that *"much study wearies the body"*[41].

The key to mastering Upside Down language is to involve Holy Trinity in your everyday life. You can share your joys, your successes, your failures, your sorrows, your troubles, your heartaches, your rejections, your loneliness, whatever it may be, with Him. If you see or hear anything funny, share the joke with Lord Jesus. If you read something you do not understand, share it with Holy Spirit, and ask for illumination. If you see or experience something in the weird and wonderful world that HF created, then let Him know what you think. I have been known to ask Him what He was thinking about when He created some of the hideous creatures on our planet, but I wisely stopped before overstepping my boundaries.

And do not forget to use your imagination. I can assure you, you have this gift because I have prayed and asked Holy Spirit to anoint everyone reading this book with this special gift.

BROTHER JAMES: Do you not think that this Upside Down language is a bit simplistic and childish?

DEBBIE: I agree that it is rather simplistic, but I would not say it is childish. Childlike would be a better word to describe it. I have the utmost respect and reverence for Almighty God and I fear Him, but it has not stopped me from loving and enjoying Him.

He freed me to be myself and relate to Him in my own unique way. If you find this language childish, then you can go ahead and do your own thing. There is room for varying expressions when it comes to your relationship with God. After all, He created us as individuals for His glory.

Addressing the class;

DEBBIE: Now to my fellow Upside Down residents, I failed to tell Almighty God that there is a cost for my taking the class, and unless all of you start speaking Upside Down language to justify my time, I shall send my bill to Holy Trinity. So, I expect to hear various renditions of Upside down. If you like you can invent your own words, but whatever the case, just speak it!

BROTHER JOHN: I like how you have made God come alive. From your experience, what would you say are the specialist areas of each person of Almighty God?

DEBBIE: You have asked a question on a favourite topic of mine and I hope you have eternity to listen.

Let us start with HF; He is the referee of heaven and earth. When He blows the whistle all activity ceases. However, His specialist area is in carrying out inquiries; He chairs all inquiry boards. This is something He has done since the time of Adam and Eve. He is an expert at fishing out things as He likes to get to the bottom of any matter. He either carries out the inquiry Himself or sends His prophets to do it on His behalf. If you doubt this about

HF take a look at the story of Adam and Eve, Cain and Abel, David and the Bathsheba-gate scandal, or even the story of Ahab and Naboth's vineyard. These are just a few cases from the bible.

HF has a knack for asking questions that get to the heart of the matter. You know that once He starts throwing in the questions you are finished; *Adam*[42], *Cain*[43], *King Ahaziah*[44] and so many others can testify to this. My advice to you: *Do not let Him carry out an inquiry into what you have done, and do not even bother getting into an argument with Him.* Just throw yourself at His mercy; admit and confess your wrongdoing because by the time it gets to the inquiry stage, you know that His disciplinary process is about to kick in. *If in doubt ask King David about the Bathsheba affair; you will find this account in the bible.*[45]

Coming back to my point, it is no use arguing with HF. I mean, if you were Cain what satisfactory answer would you give to the question, *"Where is Abel your brother?"* knowing that you have just murdered him? Or what answer would you give Elijah to take back to God if you were King Ahaziah of Samaria and were asked, *"Is it because there is no God in Israel that you have sent to enquire of Baal-Zebub the god of Ekron?"*[46]

And just in case you think you can hide from HF then you had better think twice. Here is what David had to say; *"Where can I go from Your Spirit? Or where can I flee from Your presence?"*[47] There is absolutely no place to hide in the entire universe.

SISTER BECKY: Thanks for that. I never really thought of HF in this way before. So, what about Lord Jesus?

DEBBIE: I could tell you a billion things about Lord Jesus

but you would probably not believe me. However, something I know He specialises in is managing lives. Just think of the billions of lives down the ages that have been committed to Him over thousands of years and not one was snatched from His hands.

There is no trickery or clever argument that you can use to hoodwink Lord Jesus. One gaze from Him will pierce to the very core of your being and blow apart any wisecracks you thought you had. Remember, after spending thirty three years living among mankind, He knows it all. So, if you think you can pull a fast one on Lord Jesus then you have picked on the wrong guy.

One thing you will be glad to know is that once you have made Him your Lord and Saviour you can prepare for a life time of adventure. He will make you do things you do not want to do and send you to places you do not want to go. He will even drag you kicking and screaming all the way only for you to get there and find out that it is where you should have been in the first place; and then you find yourself thanking Him.

Then, just when you think you can rest a while, He will take you on yet another adventure and the whole process will start all over again. This will repeat itself several times throughout your lifetime, and probably in eternity. If in doubt, ask Apostle Peter. I bet it never crossed his mind that when he accepted the call from Jesus to be a fisher of men he would end up as the head of the Church. If you are still not sure then let me bring it closer to home. Check out Billy Graham; when he made Jesus his Lord and saviour, he did not know that he would take the message of the gospel to the four corners of the world.

All the saints down the ages, both living and dead will back me up on this. So brace yourself and enjoy the ride. Remember that there is no need arguing with Lord Jesus. He is the one who orchestrates the events of your life and He has everything under control.

When your life starts to take funny turns that you do not comprehend just bear in mind that this could be Lord Jesus at work. Do not start binding and casting out imaginary demons, or rejecting every plan in the name of Jesus *(as some have been known to do)*. This will not alter His plan for your life. You are better off co-operating with Him and following the path He has marked out for you. This will surely be less painful.

And another thing; Lord Jesus will not settle for anything less than one hundred per cent. Anything else is simply not good enough in His book. So here is my advice to you: Commit your whole life into His loving arms for His safe keeping. After all, He will definitely do a better job with your life than you would. With Him your life is guaranteed to count for something; with Him you will achieve more and derive an immense sense of fulfilment.

BROTHER JOHN: Now that you put it that way, I can understand some things about my life that did not make sense before. So what about Holy Spirit?

DEBBIE: From my experience I would say that Holy Spirit specialises in making things supernaturally bigger; and I mean mega big! You whisper something to Him privately that pleases His heart and before you know it the whole world is in on it. I call it Holy Dove Broadcasting. Have you ever wondered how certain songs, hymns, books and other divine concepts such as The Alpha course, find their way around the world?

Another aspect of Holy Spirit is that He is very contrary. He is contrary to the flesh, to the world and to the devil. He will guide you and counsel you in ways that may not make sense to you until well after the event. But even though His ways may sometimes be painful, they are always right. I have already whinged on this, so I will not repeat myself. However, to back up my case, why not take a peep into Jeremiah's life?

The prophet Jeremiah, under the unction of Holy Spirit, had prophesied time and time again that the Babylonians would carry Judah into exile. When the prophecy finally came to pass, and while the Babylonians were attacking the gates of Jerusalem, *Holy Spirit instructs Jeremiah, who by the way is still locked up in prison, to buy a piece of land from his cousin!*[48] Hello! You are about to go into exile for seventy years, why would you want to buy land? I would have thought that the wise thing to do would be to conserve your resources in preparation for the uncertain future.

To update the story, it would be like being instructed by Holy Spirit to put your savings in *Northern Rock*[49] when it had already hit rock bottom; a time when all other sensible investors were taking their money out. You just know that you will be the only one on the queue depositing money, while the queue for withdrawals stretches for miles. Or how would you like to buy shares in a financial institution in the middle of a credit crunch, when other investors are trying to off-load theirs? Now, if this is not contrary behaviour I would like to know what is.

In fairness to Holy Spirit, if you obey Him like Jeremiah

did, you will be in for a big windfall. Just imagine if the deed to the piece of land that Jeremiah bought was found today, his descendants would be in for a good return on that investment. *(I must point out here that this was not the reason for buying the land. The land was bought as an assurance that the Israelites would once again return to occupy Judah).* So, if Holy Spirit gives you contrary counsel, just obey Him. Remember that He knows something that you do not know, and are unlikely to find out as it cannot be discerned or read in any book. I had to learn this lesson the hard way.

One last thing; Holy Spirit is the Public Relations (PR) Officer for all Christians. There is no need to promote yourself if you are walking in the path that He designed for you. Holy Spirit is excellent at PR, and I speak from personal experience. He makes the little things you do go a very long way; way beyond what you think to be possible. That is what it means to have favour with God.

Self-promotion will get you somewhere but not as far as Holy Spirit will take you if you concentrate your effort on walking in the path Lord Jesus has charted for you. If you entrust your PR to Holy Spirit, you will grow in influence way beyond your wildest dreams and go all the way to the top.

HF: I must congratulate You Holy Spirit on Your most excellent teaching methods. See how Debbie has turned out. Who would have believed it?

LORD JESUS: I agree with HF. I can see Holy Spirit has been very busy. All He needs to do now is anoint a few more Debbies and He will be able to take early retirement and concentrate on broadcasting and PR, as Debbie puts it.

HF: I do however have one concern. Is there any hiding place for Me? I mean, the way Debbie has revealed My modus operandi is a bit worrying.

HOLY SPIRIT: HF, is it not it a bit late to start looking for a hiding place? Your holy textbook, the bible has been in public domain for hundreds of years. Anyone can read it and work things out for themselves, just like Debbie. So maybe You should forget the idea of a hiding place. It simply will not work!

Holy Spirit turned to thank Debbie.

HOLY SPIRIT: Thanks Debbie for taking the class. You can go ahead and send the bill to HF.

HF: Wait a minute Holy Spirit, she takes Your class and I get to pick up the tab; nice try. How come I always end up paying all the bills?

LORD JESUS: HF I am sure that You have not run out of money or resources. I think You better settle the bill before Debbie decides to quote a few scriptures. As You very well know, she always has one or two scriptures handy to back up her case!

HOLY SPIRIT: Never You mind Jesus, as Debbie would tell HF herself, *"If You rain the money like manna from heaven into my garden, it will be acceptable"*.

Just one more thing HF, Jesus; We have to bless this book.

*And so Almighty God – Father, Son and Holy Spirit spoke with one voice along with all the angels and saints in heaven and blessed Debbie's **Diary of Upside Down Prayers**.*

DEBBIE: So there you have it my dear readers; it is an

approved text book. A must read for all Upside Down citizens! It is my first attempt at organising all the angels and saints on earth. So please join me in making it a success.

NOTES

1. **Kuku** *Nigerian Pidgin word meaning "just". It is placed in sentence for emphasis*

2. **Pikin** *Nigerian Pidgin word for "child"*

3. **Haba!** ***Hausa word for "good grief" that has become part of Nigerian Pidgin English.*

4. **Abajo** ****Yorùbá word meaning "no wonder"*

5. **Abi** *Yoruba word meaning "isn't it". It is placed in sentence for emphasis*

6. **Ewo** *****Igbo word meaning "alas"*

7. **Astralise** *Upside Down word for "astral projection"*

8. **Isaiah 42:8b**

9. **2 Corinthians 12:9b**

10. **Garri** *a processed cassava product eaten in some parts of West Africa; it can be eaten hot, in dough form, with a sauce or cold, as a cereal. When eaten as a cereal it is ideal for the water and the garri to be at approximately the same level.*

11. **Garri don pass water or water don pass garri** - *Nigerian Pidgin phrase meaning "the garri is above the level of water or the level of water is above the garri"*

12. **Abi na by force?** *Nigerian Pidgin phrase meaning "do you want to impose it on me?"*

13. **Isaiah 28:29b**

14. **Malachi 3:6**

15. **Isaiah 55:8-9**

16. **Olodo** *Yoruba word meaning one who scores 0% or "dunce"*

17. **Philippians 4:19**

18. **Bubu** *pronounced booboo, this is a loose fitting, flowing robe. (It is usually very easy to make and only an exceptionally bad seamstress would make an ill-fitting one)*

19. **Bezalel** *the artistic designer of the Tabernacle of Meeting and the Ark of the Covenant. Read more about him in Exodus 31:2, 37-39*

20. **Butu** *a respectful greeting to an elder that involves genuflecting*

21. **Akara** *also known as bean cake, it is made from skinned black-eyed or brown beans formed into a ball and then deep-fried in oil. It is suitable for vegetarians and vegans.*

22. **Moin-moin** *is made from skinned black-eyed or brown beans, seasoned and steamed. It can be adapted to suit vegetarians and vegans.*

23. **Don yamutu yakari** *Hausa phrase meaning "has been killed off"*

24. **Oghene biko** ******Urhobo phrase meaning "Lord have mercy"*

25. **Oluwa sanu** *Yorùbá phrase meaning "Lord have mercy"*

26. **Chineke mme ebele** *Igbo phrase meaning "Lord have mercy"*

27. **Okpemu** *Urhobo word meaning "serious talk or a very grave matter"*

28. **Exodus 20:13**

29. **Chei!** *Nigerian Pidgin word meaning "my goodness!" It also means "good grief!"*

30. **Wahala** *Nigerian Pidgin word meaning "trouble"*

31. **Ewo** *Igbo word meaning "alas"*

32. **Mark 7:7**

33. **Mark 7:8**

34. **Matthew 28:20**

35. **Emuakpor Oghene mhe** *Urhobo phrase meaning "there is wonder in the world my God"*

36. **See Acts 3:1-10**

37. **Philippians 2:10**

38. **Hebrews 8:1**

39. **See Romans 8:27 & 34**

40. **Matthew 18:20**

41. **Ecclesiastes 12:12b New International Version (NIV)**

42. **Genesis 3:9**

43. **Genesis 4:9**

44. **2 Kings 1:16**

45. **See 1 Kings chapters 11 and 12**

46. **2 Kings1:16**

47. **Psalm 139:7**

48. **Jeremiah 32:1-16**

49. **Northern Rock** *a UK bank that sought and received a liquidity support facility from the Bank of England following problems in the credit markets in 2007*

__Nigerian Pidgin__ is an English-based pidgin and a creole language spoken as a lingua franca across Nigeria. The language is commonly referred to as "Pidgin" or "Brokin".

**__Hausa__ is a language spoken in parts of West Africa*

***__Yorùbá__ is a language spoken in South West and Western Nigeria. It is also spoken in other parts of West Africa notably in the Republic of Benin and Togo.*

****__Igbo__ is a native language of the Igbo people, an ethnic group primarily located in south eastern Nigeria.*

*****__Urhobo__ is one of the Edoid languages and is spoken by the Urhobo people of southern Nigeria.*

APPENDIX I

IN PRAISE OF ALMIGHTY GOD:
Father, Son and Holy Spirit

HEAVENLY FATHER

Creator of the universe, The Source of all life, sovereign, holy, perfect, loving, caring, compassionate, merciful, forgiving, faithful, patient, just, impartial, the same today, yesterday and forever, complete, all-powerful, all-knowing, all-seeing, magnificent, beautiful, worthy of all praise, all honour, all glory and adoration.

LORD JESUS

Judge of the earth, Redeemer, Saviour, holy, Lamb of God who cleanses from all sin, perfect, the same today, yesterday and forever, loving, caring, compassionate, merciful, forgiving, faithful, all-powerful, all-knowing, all-wise, magnificent, Lord of lords, King of kings, Prince of peace, worthy of all praise, all honour, all glory, all power and adoration.

HOLY SPIRIT

All over the world at the same time, holy, perfect, eternal, loving, caring, compassionate, comforter, counsellor, helper, teacher, kind, glorified, all-powerful, all-wise, all-knowing, all-seeing, magnificent, beautiful, worthy of all praise, all honour, all glory, all adoration.

APPENDIX II

MAKING THE MOST OF PRAISE

1. Say the words out loud until you are familiar with them.

2. Say the words in your mind as this will help you maintain an attitude of praise.

3. Say the words lovingly from your heart because you believe them.

4. Praise relaxes and calms the mind and enables you to hear the Holy Spirit more clearly when He speaks to you. As you obey Him, you will soon see a difference in your life. When faced with a difficult situation, or tempted to worry, praise instead and you will feel the love, joy, peace and the re-assuring presence of Almighty God in a new way.

5. The praise list can be used as a tool for meditation. Take any aspect of the character of Almighty God and think about what this means to you on an individual level.

6. The praise list is not exhaustive. Treat them as key words and feel free to add and say them in any way you like.

~ Deborah Ogefere-Onyekwuluje

www.ingramcontent.com/pod-product-compliance
Lightning Source LLC
LaVergne TN
LVHW011238080426
835509LV00005B/544